SWING, WALK, REPEAT

Observations from a lifelong golf obsession.

JAY REVELL

with illustrations by Dave Baysden

Recorded in the Year 2020

BACK NINE PRESS

Back Nine Press
Chicago, Illinois
www.back9press.com
Twitter and Instagram: @backninepress

9 8 7 6 5 4 3 2 1

First Edition
Printed in the United States of America.
Book design by Asya Blue

Library of Congress Cataloging-in-Publication Data applied for.

Names: Revell, Jay, 1987– author.
Title: Swing, Walk, Repeat.
Other Titles: Observations from a lifelong golf obsession.
pages cm

ISBN 978-1-956237-02-3 (hardcover)
ISBN 978-1-956237-03-0 (e-book)

For my family –
Sarah, Winnie, John David, and Leon.
You all make me feel like the luckiest man alive.

TABLE OF CONTENTS

FOREWORD

The first time I read Jay Revell's work, he was able to do what all of my favorite writers do: he transported me. Reading Jay's 2017 essay on Pasatiempo Golf Club, I felt as if I had walked the same fairways Jay had. Mind you, I have read several articles before on Pasatiempo, but Jay's perspective and writing were different. His words made a golf course I had never played come alive in my mind's eye.

Jay writes with a certain relaxed pace and movement that I've long admired. Anyone who knows Jay's essays knows he can be found carrying his bag, walking alongside a wide range of characters that include the legendary Ed "Gramps" Bates, his colorful gang at Capital City Country Club, his ever-faithful labrador Leon, or his growing family. Whoever Jay is with, the rhythm is always that of a comfortable stroll. In the fast-paced world we choose to live in, it's good to know there are people like Jay who take the time to walk, reflect, breathe, and—thankfully—share those experiences so gracefully.

Writers will often say they feel stuck, unable to put the words together to express their vision, ideas, or emotions. Surely, you've heard of writer's block, and let me be the first to tell you: it's not a lot of fun. The creative block that writers experience can affect all parts of their lives. Sometimes we just feel overwhelmed, confused, frozen. Our synapses aren't firing as we'd like, and we aren't sure what to do. These feelings become far more common when we are chasing small children, trying to navigate work and relationships, living in a pandemic, or all of the above. Life can come at you very fast, as they say, and life is relentless. Personally, when I face uncertainty, I repeat a mantra that I have found to be extremely helpful. I ask myself, 'what is the next *best* thing I can do?' This simplifies what can seem daunting. It provides light when the path is dark. We are reminded that every process—every journey—is a collection of steps. We just need to keep taking them. As Jay set out to write *Swing, Walk, Repeat*, he was the living embodiment of that mantra. He kept swinging. He kept walking. And he kept doing it day after day.

Whether it's through news feeds or guided meditations, we are a society obsessed with small, consumable content. When Jay first told me about the format for *Swing, Walk, Repeat*, I was excited for people that would get to read small nuggets of Jay's wisdom and storytelling on a daily basis. Not because it would make you a better player or improve your swing, but my hope for you, dear reader, is that the book will touch your soul and tug at your heartstrings a little bit. If you read an observation each day with your morning coffee, my guess is you'll walk out the door and greet the world with a warmer disposition.

If you've bought this book, I'm going to assume you like to play golf. It's probably a safe bet that you're familiar with many of the elements that make the game great: natural surroundings, lasting friendships, new destinations, inspiring architecture, and exciting competition. While all of those things draw praise, the gift of Jay's writing is that he illuminates the little things, so we never forget how special they are. There is great wisdom to be found walking alone (or with our faithful dog) in the long shadows of the evening, contemplating life's questions, remembering those who taught us and those who loved us. We get the chance to reflect on why we do the things we do, why we play this game, and what the game teaches us.

Whether we find the answers to these questions doesn't really matter. What matters is that we keep asking them. We keep appreciating. We keep reflecting. We keep doing the next best thing. We never stop trying to swing, walk, and repeat.

—Laz Versalles

INTRODUCTION

January 1, 2020 was a good day. I started the year with a smile as I enjoyed a winter day at my home course, Capital City Country Club, in Tallahassee, Florida. There wasn't much golf traffic that afternoon, so I took my wife and two-year-old daughter out to go walk a few holes. We had some fun taking swings and dreaming about what the next 12 months might be like. Little did we know, the year ahead would be unlike any year any of us had ever experienced.

New Year's Day is always a time for reflection and dreaming. A golf course is a fine place to do both. I remember strolling the fairways with my family, and as evening crept up to us, I had an idea for a writing prompt. Watching my wife and daughter play near the 13th green, I took a photo of them both. We were all having such fun, and it made me think about all the little ways golf gives me joy. Later that night, as the girls went to bed, I sat down and wrote a few sentences about our experience that day.

In what became an Instagram post, I concluded my thoughts with the following line:

> **"There's a lot to love about this world, and I intend on staying busy this year, enjoying many days just like this."**

There was no way to know just how prophetic that statement was. I titled the post "Golf Story 1/365." Like many of us around the world that declare half-brained resolutions on New Year's Day, I set out to do something that would be hard to keep up with. I wanted to see if I could tell a brief, daily story about how the game shapes my life for a full calendar year. What started as a system for exercising my writing muscles turned into a diary of observations about a game that I love. A selection of those entries is now the content of this book.

I was unsuccessful in writing a post each day, but the habit I created generated well over 250 of these observations during the year. Because of the challenges that occurred throughout 2020, I cut myself some slack. As the days fell off the calendar, the world changed more and more. Both the larger reality of society and the intimate experiences of home were seemingly forever altered. That's what pandemics do.

It was in early March when we all became familiar with the virus called COVID-19. I'm no scientist so I won't dive into the particulars, but this molecular wrecking ball tore through every country on earth, and for the first time in our lifetimes, everyone on the planet was being affected by the same damn thing.

During a frantic few days that spring, the whole planet grinded to a screeching halt. The pandemic paused nearly all global commerce, and governments issued what became known as stay-at-home orders. As the virus took hold of our world, hospitals became overwhelmed and millions of people became sick or died. The deadliness of the virus inspired levels of panic and concern that were unprecedented in our time.

Here in the United States, it was an election year, and every aspect of the pandemic became fodder for politicians to hurl at each other. With the entire country sitting at home, a whole new set of problems began to emerge. What was originally forecasted to last a few weeks became a new normal that caused stress and tension to escalate for both individuals and society. Social unrest began to rise, and by summer the murder of a Black man named George Floyd sparked protests and a worldwide conversation about race relations. Tumultuous doesn't even begin to describe the mood.

On the home front, I lost my job in the fall, and my wife lost a pregnancy.

Depression was a constant threat to my sanity, and if not for one ever-present escape, I may have lost my mind. Despite all the challenges of the outside world and body blows to my own life, I still had golf.

Fortunately, where I live in Florida, golf courses were allowed to stay open during the lockdowns as a means for safe recreation. As the surges waned, various businesses reopened, and golf courses were increasingly deemed to be one of the safer places that people could spend time. Because offices were closed and work became remote, I turned to the golf course as a personal savior more than ever before. I wasn't alone, either.

Golfers around the globe flocked to the game in a way not seen in decades. As restrictions were lifted, the game flourished. The terrible virus that has killed about 5 million people worldwide and has affected so much of the world's economy somehow lifted golf from a 20-year slump.

Today, the golf industry continues to see record numbers of rounds played and equipment sold. Golf travel has come roaring back, too. This phenomenon also trickled down to a whole new generation of golf media personalities. The many golf writers, influencers, and other voices who had arisen through the game in the past decade were all well-positioned to take advantage, and many did, myself included. The COVID-19 golf boom was and remains real.

During the early days of the pandemic, when I was writing my regular golf posts, I noticed a large uptick in readership and engagement with what I was sharing. These daily musings became a meaningful way for me to connect with golfers old and new around the globe. I received messages, notes, and emails about the words I was sharing, and it convinced me that my posts may just be worthy of a book.

I wrote my first book, *The Nine Virtues of Golf*, in the years preceding the pandemic. It actually launched in June 2020. The success of that essay collection—along with the outreach I was receiving with my daily posts—was all the convincing I needed that my brand of storytelling indeed has an audience. I'm not sure how many folks my words are reaching, but I do know that they have meant a lot to some. Every response became the fuel I needed to push through the pandemic, do my work, and chase my golf-writing dreams.

Those same messages were helpful when I decided to start my own business late in 2020. Hearing that people were moved by my words gave me the confidence to use them for purposes beyond just golf. I launched a small marketing and public relations firm in October, and now my career and golf writing passion seem to be more aligned than ever.

As 2020 waned, I found myself starting to see the whole year as a bit of a twisted blessing. Once the temperatures dropped and the days got short again, I began going back and reading the golf posts I had written from earlier in the year. Because of how the pandemic steered me to the course more than any other year in my adult life, I was able to fully reflect on all the ways golf has impacted my existence. All those days walking with my dog, laughing with friends, watching my family blossom, and chasing low scores made me realize just how much golf has made me who I am.

I'm now pleased to share those golf writings in the form of this book. With the help of my friend Jim Sitar at Back Nine Press, I was able to turn my musings into a collection of miniature essays on the game. Designed to be read as a golf devotional of sorts, I like to think that you can pick up this volume, open it to any page, and find some words that reflect why golf is such a special game to so many.

In these pages, you'll find reflections on how I like to play, the friendships golf inspires, and how the game has been an essential part of my family. I included passages that document lessons I've been taught, truths I've discovered, and emotions I've experienced. There are even some ramblings on what I think about the current state of the game and how it operates as a business. In many ways, this is my golf manifesto.

2020 was a year that shook up everything in my life. The world has likely been permanently changed by those 12 months, too. I'd like to think that golf came out ahead in 2020, but we will all have to wait and see what transpires in the years to come. Either way, the game gave me something wonderful to focus on when life got really challenging, and I'm glad I stopped to write those feelings down.

Looking back, I can't help but think that 2020 was a lot like the golf rounds I play. It began with high hopes, saw early promise, faltered in the middle, and looked bleak for some time. But finally, after a late charge, the last putt dropped for a decent score, and I was smiling, eager to go out once again.

I hope you enjoy reading this book as much as I enjoyed putting it together. If you love golf, I imagine you'll like what you find in the pages that follow. I'm hopeful that at least it leaves you optimistic about how the game can keep you moving along when times get tough. I've yet to find a problem that can't be sorted out with a long walk and a few swings. What you are about to read is proof of that.

This is Swing, Walk, Repeat.

Cheers,
-Jay

A LOVE FOR GOLF

A friend of mine mentioned to me recently that he could tell golf made me happy, because I always show my smile while on the course. As he noted, the game does indeed bring me great joy and has long contributed to my jolly disposition.

The game of golf simply brings the best out of me. Isn't that why we all play… to tap into our best selves?

For me, golf represents a constant search for improvement. That being said, it's certainly a wonderful feeling to be on the golf course, and I tend to believe that any day spent chasing the glory of golf is a day well lived.

On the golf course I find that I am closer to nature, myself, and even God. A walk on the course is a prolonged meditation. I find my most honest thoughts and truest feelings while playing. Over the course of my golfing life, I have discovered a great deal of inner peace through chasing a little white ball across the countryside.

Honestly, what's not to love? I'm hooked on the game because it makes me happy. That has placed me on a nonstop search for as much joy as I can find. Along my journey, I continue to find new ways that golf makes me smile. I think I'll keep at it.

PERSIMMON

Those of you over 40: you remember persimmon woods, don't you?

For generations, this soft lumber was artfully crafted into club heads the world over, and it was the hallmark of a game that was once all about precision.

Today golf is much different, and so are its tools.

The sharp crack of persimmon striking a ball can still be heard in some places. Those who find joy in playing with these forgotten beauties know that a persimmon swing is different than one for metals. Where most 21st-century swings are built to crush the ball, a persimmon swing was fashioned for contact.

The feeling that occurs when this wooden club head connects to its spherical target is as heavenly as it is unique.

Swinging these clubs can make you a better player and certainly a more appreciative one. Knowing what the game used to be like is a useful way to improve how to play it today. Persimmons don't translate well to all forms of golf, but in many places, players would benefit by using these clubs from time to time.

I find great joy in collecting wooden clubs, and even more pleasure from playing with them. When I go to grab my clubs, the choice between metal and persimmon isn't always easy. The more I select the persimmon game, the more I'm inclined to do it again. The opportunity to feel the impact in my fingers and hear the magical sound echo through the course has almost become a delicacy. As my relationship with golf continues to evolve, I find myself ordering persimmon from the menu more and more.

GRAMPS

There is no sweeter swing than that of my grandfather's.

Gramps has a classical technique. His turn is rhythmic and smooth, creating a motion that moves as gentle as clouds moving across the sky. Within his seemingly effortless swing are 85 years of ball striking experience. He still thinks like a shot maker and his game is a reflection of a life lived in and around the game.

Gramps has given me much to emulate over the years, and I'm hopeful to have just as many rounds to discover my swing as he has.

Each time we play, I learn something new. His clever takes on golf and simple swing tips are like breadcrumbs for me to follow. They're clues that someday, if I'm lucky, will help lead me to a swing as pretty as his is.

" Each time we play, I learn something new "

GOLF JUNK

I'm running out of room for my golf gear. This war is being fought on two fronts, and the odds of winning look increasingly slim.

As many men have experienced, I have been slowly losing space every day since I met my wife. Once I had a house filled with golf treasures, and ever since we started dating, I've been gradually losing that ground.

I'm not complaining, though. I need a wonderful woman to stop my hoarding tendencies, and fortunately I have the best one in the world. That same woman is also the person I love building a family with. Which means that it won't be long before the space I have left likely becomes lost to time and toddlers.

I've still got a wall in the garage filled with clubs. These sticks aren't just for show. I still play with them! It's fun to mix up which equipment I want to use.

I've got a little bit of everything and not nearly enough room to keep it all. The play set for my daughter, a stroller, new washing machine, and many baby-related items that we are saving for "the next one" have all encroached into my little corner. What once was curated in a museum-like setting is now crammed in various golf bags, tucked in behind the water heater.

This is my stage in life. The only aspect of the game shrinking faster than my allotted time to play is the space I need to keep my golf junk. Someday soon I'm sure I'll have to haul much of it away to someplace else. The big question will be whether I tell my wife about the storage unit.

GROWING UP WITH GOLF

A golf course is a great place to be a teenager. It's the sort of environment most adolescents need as they begin the transition to adulthood.

During one's formative years, it's important to have a laboratory for learning. I can hardly imagine anything more suited to that than golf. Every hole is an opportunity to discover something new about life.

Golf teaches many things that young people will benefit from knowing: patience, perseverance, self-belief, gratitude, and courteousness. Playing with contemporaries and other acquaintances strengthens friendships and creates conversational skills. Golf reveals a certain grit, too. It's also a fine sport for developing personality and character.

Teenagers tend to think they know a lot, but their hours spent failing at golf will prove otherwise. It's good to be humbled regularly in a safe environment, and golf will do that with ease. Young people need places for exploring who they are. A long walk in pursuit of a perplexing game does just the trick.

Teenagers long for freedom, and a golf course can offer that in a way that works for both them and their guardians. There's just enough room to roam without becoming lost. A golfer is a good thing to be, and the teenage years are a fine time to become one.

TRAVELING FOR GOLF

The trouble with traveling for golf is that I keep finding new places to love. The worst part? After falling for them, I find myself worried I may never see them again.

Have you ever played a golf course that you truly struggled to depart from?

Throughout my adventures I've found a few such places for which it still hurts to think about. These are the courses that occupy the corners of my memory and have maintained a strong hold on my heart.

I find myself thinking about them as if they were a long-lost lover, surely the result of some soulful connection I made there with the game.

In some cases, I've only played the course once, but the round lives on through my vivid recollections. I remember the colors of the sky and the contours of the ground: visual feasts that once devoured become memories forever chiseled in the bedrock of my mind.

Having to leave an experience of this magnitude is painful, but the idea of never returning is damn near unbearable. Photos from these travels trigger both smiles and sighs. It's easy to drift off to a daydream and get lost in plots that would help me make it back.

Sadly, the odds of a second trip are slim, and despite loving one stop so dearly, there are an endless number of new places to see. I must instead venture to new destinations in hopes of finding the next unforgettable course.

FEEL PLAYER

I have always been a feel player. The game doesn't make sense to me any other way.

My swing doesn't work in some textbook fashion either. Instead, it twists and bends in accordance with the ways I've had to tweak it over the years.

I keep the clubface shut throughout the backswing. The club comes over the line and off plane, too. I make a good turn, but it leaves me in an odd place. However, on the way down, I get my hands back into a good position as I rip my hips left of the target line. With open shoulders and a lagging clubface, I pull my way into the strike. All of this produces a cut spin.

From the moment the ball is struck, it takes off left of my aim point before fading back to the intended destination. I swing down through the ball, taking large divots that are the result of a steep angle of descent. Finishing well, but often abbreviated. My method for distance control.

When it works as intended, I'm a fairway finder and pin seeker. When it's off, I'm as lost as any old duffer.

The only way to keep this motion held together is to go back to the same method I used to build it: practice.

This swing of mine was born beneath the heat of summer and the shade of a pecan tree. Long days on the range with a broken-down picker and all the balls I could hit. That's where I found what worked for me.

Today, that pecan tree is gone, and my time for practice is short, but I still know how to feel for what's right. Even in smaller doses, it's through reps that I find my groove again.

No cameras, no teachers, no monitors. Just me and my senses in search of a certain feeling that I keep stored deep inside my golf-crazed heart.

BAD WEATHER, NO BOTHER

Golfers don't mind bad weather. Rain, cold, heat, wind: it doesn't matter. They just want a chance to play. As long as there's a game, golfers will show up. That takes love. That requires commitment. Maybe a little crazy, too.

That's the hold golf has on people. This sport breeds a desire for which there's no ultimate satisfaction. Swings must be taken in order to calm the soul. No forecast can stop that. The round goes on, no matter the elements.

" That takes love. That requires commitment "

RESPECTING THE COURSE

It's amazing the number of signs we need to have in golf. "Fill divots", "no carts", and "Please repair ball marks" to name a few.

They speak to us in simple direct language and don't mince words, yet every day people walk by and ignore them.

Come on golfers. Let's get it together, shall we?

It costs a fortune to maintain a golf course, and so many of us just make it harder for these places to stay open. Then there are the entire teams of people that work hard to bring courses to life. The turf and maintenance teams at our courses deserve our admiration, respect, and certainly acknowledgement via behavior. Yet still there are catalogs—literal catalogs—full of signs aimed at reducing foolish acts on the course.

We need to do better.

There may only be a small lot that are the worst offenders, but we all have our moments. There's no excuse: all of us should become better examples for others in showing respect for the course.

Fill your divot and a few more. Keep your cart—if you must drive one—on the path. If you see a ball mark, fix yours and others near you.

Think of a world in which we don't need signs, where our experiences are universally improved. We all have a small role to play. You never know who is watching, and good acts of golf culture can be contagious. Let's be the change we know we need to see and show the golfing world we care. If you love something so much, showing some respect should be easy.

No signs necessary. Perhaps we can someday earn the privilege of not needing such ridiculous direction.

DOGS AND GOLF

My labradoodle Leon and I make a good pair for many reasons. One of which is that we can easily enjoy the solitude of an empty golf course.

Our best times together occur in the hours just before sundown while walking over golf holes we know by heart. We both have our favorite foot paths that we prefer to traverse, but those divergent routes lead to similar experiences. In this—our favorite routine—we both get to let our guard down and escape our regular burdens.

I enjoy the walk because I get to connect with both nature and my deepest thoughts. He enjoys the walk for the opportunity to explore vast lands while unencumbered by leash or fence. The stroll does us both a whole world of good.

For years we would walk around town for this variety of exercise. That was until I joined a club and began testing the boundaries of acceptance for dogs on the property. Fortunately for us both, the club couldn't care less about us enjoying the course together.

So, for the past few years, we've made this ritual our habit. It's during our walks together that we've come to know each other better than ever before. There's no way to hide who you are on a golf course, and even if you could, a dog would sniff out the truth.

Leon and I share in a most enjoyable existence while walking over these hills together. Over those many adventures we've grown quite close, and I can't help but feel that golf has helped us better understand one another. I suppose that's the point of the game, though. That being just one of the many things I've learned about life and golf from a dog. I think I'll keep him and hope he'll keep me. We just work well together, and golf is a good reminder of that.

GOLF THAT STARTS WITH YES

Struggling golf courses that are looking to find new customers should learn to say yes more. Stuffy clubs in need of modern sensibilities should as well. There's a vibrant and thriving scene emerging in the game today, and it's rooted in a deep love for the simple joys of golf.

Players are seeking places that celebrate friendship, fun times, and spirited competition. For most places, facilitating such an environment requires a shift in attitude.

Saying yes to golfers' desire to have fun is a good way to build a strong foundation. Encouraging good times on and off the course is essential to fostering a desirable golf culture. The easiest way to create this is to listen for what the customer wants.

It's a simple recipe and one that can surely be modified to taste. This way of managing a golf experience seems to be catching on, and perhaps as more places say yes to fun and free flowing golf, that ethos will only spread further. It's proving to be a successful approach. *Yes* is a good answer to most golf questions.

THE GRILL ROOM

I was made for the grill room.

Give me the shadowy haunts painted in rich colors with dark wood trims and the sound of banter rising before sundown. It's in these places that I am home.

I was raised in this most boisterous of environments. Taught the ways of a raconteur from a young age I developed the gift of gab and later the thirst of an Irishman. My ears rejoice at the sound of gut-splitting jokes, wise cracks, nicknames, and tall tales from the course. Count me among those who know too much about golf and too little about the rest of the world.

I like my post-round settings served straight up, with little fuss and lots of soul. Burgers, fries, dogs, sammies, wings, and beer should always be plentiful. Cold beer and stiff whiskey, too.

Dress code requirements needn't be strict, but wearing a smile is strongly encouraged. If you can't bring one with you, at least take one when you go.

You'll find me in these taverns and tap rooms alongside friends both old and new. I'll be there where I belong, tucked into a table-side conversation, enjoying myself and carrying on, relishing the world I've so fortunately found myself in again.

" wearing a smile is strongly encouraged "

Right where I am meant to be.

THE PACKAGE AT THE DOOR

We get a lot of packages at my house. All kinds of orders arrive in boxes of many sizes. Between me and my wife, there's almost always something at the door waiting for us when we get home.

My wife sometimes gets new and shiny boxes with colorful labels from Amazon and other outlets. I get beat up old boxes filled with secondhand goods from eBay. Usually, Sarah's deliveries include clothes for Winnie or some kitchen gadget. My packages are of course golf-related. I get persimmon drivers, course design books, and obscure trinkets that become part of my growing collection of golf stuff.

When my wife and I pull up from work and both see a package on the porch, we are both eager to learn who it's for. It's a Christmas morning kind of thing. Walking up to the door, we both look for evidence of who the latest box may be addressed to. It's often hard to tell until we get close, but on certain delightful occasions a long slender shape is a dead giveaway that my newest club has arrived.

I never get tired of coming home to these deliveries. With a new box also comes the arrival of some item I am bound to love and enjoy while playing the best game in the world. I wonder what might arrive tomorrow.

THE GOLF BOND

My uncle likes to say that golf is much more about the people you play with than anything else. I tend to agree with him.

Among the many amazing aspects of golf, there may be nothing more important than the time the game allows us to spend with others. Golf is for making memories with family, laughing with friends, and befriending new acquaintances. I can think of no other game that offers this reward so consistently.

Golf provides for a certain nearness between players. On the course it's easy to let your guard down and engage with your fellow golfer. The game reveals how we are all vulnerable in this world, and from that realization comes empathy and understanding.

This is how we bond.

Through golf we have an open window into those we walk and play beside. Regardless of the state of any relationship, this game is a way to mend troubles and find common ground. Above all else, golf creates just the right amount of space and time for people to appreciate and enjoy each other. What a special game we have.

this game is a way to mend troubles and find common ground

RITUALS

The best golf days end with some sort of personal ritual. Golfers are crazy like that.

For me, when I've had a memorable round, I save the ball and make a small note on it explaining why. This ritual has been triggered by a variety of great golf experiences in my life.

I've kept balls that denote career-best scoring rounds, incredible shots, and even tournament victories. There are some from bucket list courses and others from when I simply played with someone special. Golf is a game with an endless potential for making memories, and for me the used balls I keep on the shelf are living proof.

Sometimes I'll spread them out and read the notes I scribbled as a means for recalling good days gone by. As I hold them in my hand, I can still sense the magic left over from rounds I'll never forget.

I don't add to this collection often. The honor of staying on the shelf is largely reserved for the very best of moments from my relationship with golf.

Some years see multiple entries to this mini hall of fame, and other stretches result in no new additions. That's the thing about golf: you never know when your game will yield something rare.

That's why when I do have a day worth remembering, I save the ball as a small memento of the glory that can be found in the game. Each time I begin a new round there's a fleeting moment in which I pull a ball from my bag to play with, look at it for a few seconds, and consider the possibilities of what the day may bring. Sometimes that ball even makes it up on the shelf.

OFFICE PUTTING

Somewhere on a video conference call right now, there are men and women going off screen and rolling putts across their carpeting with a grin on their face. Hitting the mute button while on the line is key, as the sound of a ball hitting a baseboard is always a dead giveaway.

Office putting is escapism at its very best.

No other game lends itself to such shenanigans while on the job. The seasoned office putting champion knows the breaks in the floor by heart and has mastered the art of lag putting to the wall. For those who work in golf-averse settings, this small dose of the game can help keep you sane.

It would be a stretch though to call these high jinks. It's more of a means for experimenting with your waggle or getting creative with your grip. There's no pressure to cause a bad stroke, and surely this carefree exercise is exempt from the yips.

Picking up a club while considering the business of the day can even be meditative. What could be better for making a decision or considering plans and projects than the deep thinking that comes from tinkering with your stroke?

The office putting green is a controlled environment. There's no grain or outside elements to disrupt the ball's path to the target, but email notifications can certainly cause a disturbance. Just try not to let your coworkers see your arms raised as you make the putt to win the Masters for the 10,000th time. Although, what could it hurt? They already know you're crazy.

"this small dose of the game can help keep you sane"

BEST JOB EVER

The best job I ever had was working on a golf course. I didn't know it at the time, but having a job on the maintenance team at my home club was one of the most important experiences of my life.

It was during those long summer days of my adolescence that I discovered a new depth for my love of golf. In the barn before sunrise each morning, I always arrived with some anticipation for the day ahead.

The work was sublime in that the simple, repeatable schedule gave me many hours to contemplate the world I was growing up into. Our quaint nine-hole course seemed like the most important piece of ground on earth to me. My whole life was based around that golf course, and once I began working to take care of it, my entire outlook on the game changed.

Your perspective as a player shifts dramatically when you are the one mowing the greens. Beyond the intoxicating charm of being the first person on the course each morning, my favorite part of the job was making those greens look perfect. In my teenage mind, I may as well have been the Superintendent at Augusta National.

I have vivid memories of laying the mower blades down over the wet grass and disturbing the morning dew. The pattern was repetitive yet never boring, and each day brought an opportunity to better my craft. I never thought of making a career of it, but there are some days when I wish I did.

On the maintenance staff I learned to love the golf course like it was my own child. In many ways it was.

Those hot days on the greens mowers, bush hog, and sprayer were not always easy, but man was it worth it. I often wonder if I could go get my old job back, although now I may be willing to pay them for the opportunity.

Of all the things I learned in my summers working on the course, the most important was developing a respect and admiration for those who present the course each day. Because I did the work, I can never go another round without thinking of those who make golf possible. The hard working and tireless folks that mow greens, cut fairways, and wield weed eaters are the unsung heroes of golf. I'll never forget what it was like to work alongside them, and I'll always treasure the memories of those summers.

TAKE A WALK

"Let's take a walk, shall we?" What a warm and pleasant greeting to hear from a friend.

A walk on the golf course is one of the great benefits of life. There's no better way to enjoy the good company of friends while wrapped in the surroundings of the natural world. For those inflicted with a deep love for the game, it's awfully hard to turn down an invitation for good golf, and a brisk walk with close friends. Each shared outing only leads to scheming for the next.

Golf is a gorgeous way to convene with friends in a sporty fashion, and I for one can't get enough. Take a walk? We shall indeed.

"PUTT-PUTT"

I never realized how simple golf can be until I began teaching the game to a child.

Hit the ball with the club. Get the ball in the hole. That's it.

My three-year-old daughter gets these things, and oddly enough watching her learn reminds me of the simple nature of my favorite game. Winnie still has a long way to go, but she certainly understands the basics.

There's no telling whether she'll want to play when she grows up, but right now she does. That means when she says "putt-putt," I'm quick to jump up and go.

I'm going to keep hitting that little white ball with her for as long as she will let me. No matter where the game falls in her life, I'll always be ready to go to the course with my favorite golfer, any-time she wants.

I've got a feeling that she's still got a lot to show me out there.

HALF SETS

Sometimes all you need is a half set of clubs.

I usually opt for just the even-numbered irons and a couple of woods. Over the past few years, I've found that this configuration is perfectly suited for morning walks with friends and evening strolls before sundown.

My dad has always been big on this small bag mentality, and I'm glad I finally came around. There are so many days when I only have a short window of time for golf, and the half set makes it easier to maximize those opportunities.

Reducing options makes for quick decisions and a faster pace. The less time I spend debating club choice, the more holes I can play. There's also a challenge to playing with fewer clubs. I find it to be good practice for shotmaking and a rewarding exercise for distance control.

At my home club, a half set often allows me the chance to play from places that are foreign to my normal game. It keeps things interesting. I always learn something new.

Not to say that a full set is boring, but with a half set there are seldom stock yardages. Instead, each shot is a unique construct, and I'm usually best served by playing with feel.

I recommend taking seven or eight clubs and giving it a try. The game isn't intended to be restricted to certain norms. Instead, we should all strive to step confidently outside the box. A half set is a fine way to find a new appreciation for your clubs and a fresh perspective on your game.

The game isn't intended to be restricted to certain norms

STUCK

We all get stuck sometimes. Jammed up, if you will.

The trick to making it out is to not give up: just keep swinging until you find your way. In that sense, life and golf have a funny way of resembling each other.

This is especially true when you consider the concept of a hazard. There are always traps along the way to glory, and sooner or later we all find ourselves in a precarious position. It's so easy to lose sight of hope when our fortunes seem buried in the sand, but if we are willing to keep at it, we can find our way back in play.

That doesn't mean your final score won't be affected. If you stay in the game long enough you will undoubtedly post some big numbers.

That doesn't matter, though.

It's more important to remember that you landed in a bad lie because you believed you could pull off a big shot. We all have a miss here and there, and despite coming up short on occasion, you have to believe that the next shot will be the one that turns it all around. Even though things may appear desperate, there's still a chance that something special may happen.

You never know when you will hit your next shot of a lifetime, but if you lose faith, you won't find out. Just because you landed in the junk doesn't mean you can't still win big. Swing away and see what happens next.

A PECULIAR LOT

Golfers are a peculiar lot. What is it about hitting a little white ball that drives people to act in such strange ways?

What a deprived bunch we are.

There are few obstacles that can keep a golfer from seeking out the dopamine rush that can only be found from striking the ball solidly. Those who don't play the game will never understand.

Bad weather? No worry. Going broke? So what. Relationship issues? Who cares. Legal troubles? Let's hit it. The siren of the greens calls to us constantly, and even the quietest of whispers can lure us in for more.

The simple pleasures found in a good walk, a made putt, or a daring recovery trigger intense reactions that result in long lasting psychological effects. Despite golf's ability to derail our lives, we keep pressing for more.

Our often unforgivable behavior is the result of an addiction for which there is no cure. We are a wanting breed and a silly gang. The game we love so dearly is often a detriment to our very existence, but we keep coming back again and again. All for a hope that we might hit one shot squarely on the screws.

Whatever it takes to get back to that moment is believed to be worth the sacrifice to find it. At least to a golfer, that is.

Do we stand a chance in this world? Only time will tell. Until then, you can find us at the course, trying to stir up a game or even playing alone, no matter the conditions and details be damned. The golfer will be going out again.

GOLF AND SAND

Golf and sand have a special relationship. This granular ingredient of the game is as essential to good golf as grass is.

Sand is easy to shape for course builders and when presented properly is a signature element in the world's best courses. So much more than a material for building castles at the beach, sand is an integral part of golf and will always be sought as an indication that the game could be built well in a particular place.

Sand is the foundation for firmness and is chiefly responsible for proper playing conditions. Some places are blessed with an abundance of this miraculous material, while others have to haul it in from off site.

Sand makes for well-drained land and distinctive hazards. While it may cause headaches for many a player, it also can be a beautiful and stirring component to a golf course. What was a naturally occurring landform on the links of the United Kingdom has been repeatedly added to nearly every playing ground for the game on earth.

While obviously trying to avoid sand, golfers are continuously drawn in by the risk of taking it on in a bunker or waste area. What a devilish aspect for course design. That being said, we still seek out sand for its intrigue and beauty. It still terrifies me from time to time, but on occasion sand can be a welcomed sight. Golf was invented in the sand dunes, and the game will forever flourish in the areas where it's most frequently found. Golf and sand are a match too good to be ignored. They're simply a perfect complement to each other.

NEVER SURRENDER

In golf you've got to fight till the end.

If you play this game for any time at all, you'll find a new appreciation for getting knocked on your ass. Don't stop getting back up.

Stay in the ring. That's the key to the game. Sometimes the best moments in golf come on the days when the course is winning. It only takes one shot to turn a tough day into the memory of a lifetime.

If things go south, turn your eyes back north. If you get hit in the mouth, laugh it off. If you send one in the pond, fish it out. There's no rule that you have to get upset. Just keep playing. Swing, walk, repeat.

The next shot is always the most important. In golf, you never know what may happen next. Press on. Glory won't find you in retreat.

There's no rule that you have to get upset. Just keep playing

SOUVENIRS

When I travel for golf, I always like to bring home a souvenir or two. The pro shops and gift stores may have many nice items, but I'd rather rummage through the inventory of an antique dealer or thrift peddler nearby. That's where the real treasures are found.

Instead of a logo ball, headcover, towel, or bar ware, I'd much rather have some small piece of local history.

I'm attracted to the relics that seem to have a story. Often the history of an item isn't readily available, so along with my purchase I take the liberty of searching out the past. Playing detective after the trip is a big part of the fun.

Sometimes I buy golf memorabilia, and other times I look for signs and other local flair. There are so many unique places in the American golf landscape, and no two regions are the same. Finding some small element of a place's history or culture is my favorite way to memorialize my golf trips.

These pieces I've collected while traveling make for more than just conversation starters though: they also serve as a tangible representation of a trip I took to someplace special. For me, it's about bringing home something from far away, as a means of staying close to where I've been.

EVOLUTION

The game of golf is always evolving. Across the history of this sporting pursuit, there have been numerous technological changes which have shifted norms and customs over time.

Dealing with change isn't a new phenomenon in golf, but today it seems as if the game can't quite catch up. The companies who make our clubs are seeking to sell the best equipment possible within the rules. Courses and clubs are trying and failing to stay ahead of those advances. Meanwhile, our ruling bodies have let things go a bit too far.

This has left our game in a precarious position. It's impossible to deny that this latest generation of golf equipment has created an increasingly large disparity in distance achievements between everyday amateurs and elite players.

The common golfers should not be punished for this. At the same time, the best players who are enjoying unprecedented benefits from technology may well need to see some equipment tweaks.

Maybe that means smaller clubheads and balls with more spin. I don't pretend to have all the answers, but it's obvious that something needs to be done to curb the continued increase in distance at the top levels of the game.

In baseball, the pros use different equipment than those who play at every other level of the game. It may be time to test that concept in golf.

Distance should be rewarded but done so proportionately to the rest of the game. The game we know today doesn't seem to do that.

Perhaps the USGA and other governing bodies will set a new course aimed at making golf a more equitable game between the world's best and most ardent players. I, for one, prefer a more intimate game on a shorter course and often play with persimmons. That being said, there are some courses that are even becoming less of a challenge to mid-level players like me, and that is a shame.

Golfers should be stewards of the game, and these days there's much evidence that we have ignored a problem to the point of no return. Only time will tell if we get it right from here.

WAITING FOR SPRING

The last days of winter are particularly challenging for us golfers. These are the times in which we eagerly wait for spring. There's a lingering anticipation for longer days and warmer rays of sunshine.

As the world around us is reborn, our golf swings follow suit. From the cocoon of winter there emerges a refreshed excitement for the game and hope for new-found glory. Each day that passes on the calendar brings us—the golfing population who collectively suffer while our pastime is in hibernation—just a bit closer to the walks we've missed so much.

Yet this time passes slowly in the prison cell of winter, as our thoughts continue to drift toward the golf we so badly want to play. The daydreams start to hurt, and the longing is persistent. It's okay though: spring will be here soon, and with it comes a healing prescription for our soul.

For those who must go without and others who miss its charm, golf will be back in bloom before we know it. As my grandfather used to say, it won't be as long as it has been. We just need to wait a little bit longer.

" it won't be as long as it has been "

A BAD RAP

Sometimes it feels like golf gets a bad rap.

Often lumped in with all sorts of bad behavioral traits, our game seems to be considered a nuisance by many. Sure, there are a few undesirable activities that populate the world's golfing grounds, but the gambling, drinking, swearing, and club tossing aren't representative of the broader game.

No doubt that the golfers are complicated, but should they be labeled a misfit? I think not!

Society needs golfers so that the rest of the population can look sane. Every so often there's talk of closing courses, and the list of grievances against golfers is unrolled once again. What a tiresome fuss.

The game was famously banned in Scotland for a time in an effort to eliminate distractions from the soldiers, but we all know how that turned out. We will always find a way to pursue the pleasures of our preferred pastime. Instead of putting down our ancient game, why not come in and take a few swings with us?

Golf is only a danger and a detriment if you let it be so. For hundreds of years golf has spread across the known world and has reshaped many a sporting culture. The game requires much more than anyone can offer it, yet every serious player on the planet is desperate to try. Surely anything as addicting as this can't be bad for you.

How did we golfers come by such a poor reputation? Barred from practice in parks, relegated to increasingly shrinking windows of time, and restricted to days away from work and sometimes family, the game faces many challenges.

Some folks choose not to see the beauty but instead dwell on golf's shortcomings. Should we seek to sway them or just keep playing and forget the consequences? Count me among both camps, but if I must choose, give me the latter.

A QUEST

Every golfer is on a quest of some kind. Most are in the pursuit of scores, some seek out special courses, and many are just in search of themselves. Just as no two courses are the same, individual pursuits within golf are wildly varied.

Golfers may chase championships, go after awards, or even try to hunt down history. On the opposite end of the spectrum, there are players who only care about finding good friends, having some laughs, or contributing in the local charity scramble.

There are also a seemingly endless amount of small goals in the game that we can pursue. Fairways hit, greens in regulation, and putts made are all worthy statistics for tracking progress in the game.

Some journeys are started by collecting scorecards, pro shop merch, or memorabilia. There are those seeking to make art in golf: writing, painting, and photography come to mind. There are golfers trying to shoot their age, find their swing, or perhaps pass it down to a child. There are high school players trying to make the team, club players who want to win a member-guest flight, and pros working to keep their job. Some just want to see the ball get airborne, while others are out to break 80 or 90.

The reasons that inspire people to play golf are endless and universal. Because every player on the planet is on some sort of quest, the game remains infinitely interesting.

What golf quest are you on?

FINGERPRINTS

Every golf swing is different. The ways in which we strike the ball are as unique as our fingerprints.

There's no right or wrong way to play the game, and that truth is reflected most by the infinite variety of golf swings in the world. For as long as the golf swing has been studied, there have been varied theories on how to best play the game. The best teachers are often those who can show a player how to optimize the swing they already have.

The key to playing good golf is to find a repeatable motion. The golfer who can find their best swing, time and time again, is the one to beat.

We are all in search of that one true swing: the one we can replicate often for lower scores. We should all admire the golfer who plays within their ability while being an everyday champion for the game.

The swings we make are our way of experiencing the golfing world. Each golfer is different, but the drive to improve is what brings us together.

THE BASIS FOR ADDICTION

There are only a few seconds between the striking of a golf shot and the ball coming to rest. Somehow, in that small amount of time, there are hundreds of thoughts that race through the mind of a golfer.

Could be good! Needs to go. Sit down! Please keep fading.

Turnover! Stay in bounds. Don't go in there.

This could be the one. Come on! Snuggle for me baby.

One time! Please give me a bounce…

These are just some of the phrases that populate a player's inner monologue. The reactions to a shot begin at the moment of impact and will dance all over the spectrum depending on the flight of the golf ball.

Each shot begins with a tremendous amount of hope, but things change once the ball begins its journey to the target. Sometimes our hopes are dashed, but on many occasions the results are quite positive. There are even moments when a golfer becomes convinced that they truly can command the ball at will.

It's best to keep a quiet mind, but as any golfer can tell you, there's no sense in refusing to talk to your ball. After all, we need all the help we can get. As the ball sails through the sky, screams across the ground, stretches over a hazard, or glides gently on top of the turf, there's always a plethora of possible outcomes. Anyone who plays golf can attest to the scatter plot of rushed and hectic reactions that occur with every shot.

In truth, it's those hopeful yet insecure thoughts that make the game so wildly entertaining. A big swing, the holding of a breath, and the rambling thoughts that come next are all part of why golf remains a popular game. Like any form of entertainment, golf is dependent on the regular stimulation of those who play. For the golfer, that payoff occurs in the suspension of seconds between a stroke and its result. We simply can't get enough of those hectic moments. It's the basis for our addiction.

QUIRK

I'm all in on golf's quirky side. Give me the courses with blind shots, odd customs, and strange elements. The weirder the better.

I prefer the off the beaten path, under the radar, and nearly forgotten places who have held onto the charming aspects of how the game once was. I like scrappy, one-of-a-kind environments that have features that can't be found in the mainstream. I want to aim at a painted rock, take an elevator to the next tee, walk through dusty tunnels, and ring bells to signal my progress through the course. Sign me up for those most peculiar of rituals.

My desire is to search them out and revel in their faded glory. I'll take the rough edges and rusted bridges along with the leaning buildings and chipped paint. Wear and tear never looked better than on a unique golf course. I want my golfing entrées marinated in the curious and served with a side of patina. Scoring is fun, but searching out the oddities of an aging links remains my most favorite aspect of the game.

When given the chance to choose between the modernly mundane components of most American golf facilities and some aging beauty with a good story, I'll take the latter every time. Long live the strangeness of golf. I can't get enough of it.

"Long live the strangeness of golf"

THE LOCKER ROOM

I've seen some awfully nice locker rooms in my years of playing golf, but none of them can touch the one from my old home course.

You see, I grew up in that room. It was where I first observed the old men playing cards and laughing at each other. I cashed out my first golf bets at those tables and smuggled a beer or two out of coolers as a teen. I learned all kinds of things about the world while soaking up the conversations between those cinder block walls.

That kind of education seems long extinct now. There was trash talking during rain delays and changing shoes before high school matches. When my grandad was the pro there, I helped him close for the night by locking the backdoor. Later I even had my own key. I miss the sound of old metal spikes on the terrazzo floor, and I can still hear the voices of the towering men I looked up to as a child.

That little room has had a big effect on my life. It will always be a special place for me. No matter where I go for my golf, I'll never find a place where I'm more at home with the game.

ADVENTURE

What is it about golf that makes us want to play across adventurous landforms? There are numerous aspects of the game which are worthy of pursuit, but the one that creates the longest lasting obsession is the hunt to play in new and strange lands.

The most impressive architects both understand and find inspiration in this adventure. There's an incredible art to building a proper golf hole, much less 18 of them, and the best designs are the product of a strong vision to create a memorable experience.

The golfer wants to play in places that will stand out from a lifetime of memories. The more you travel, see, and play, it only makes it more difficult for a place to be remembered for long. The high-minded course designer is always seeking the opportunity to create something beautiful, but the most lauded of the bunch are those that take some gambles with their work.

Not every course can be a hit, though, nor should they be. Architects learn as they build and are driven to create new ideas that are continually enticing to golfers. Every designer wants to build golf holes that use remarkable, natural features that draw in the attention of a player and won't let go. We all want holes that stimulate our senses and stir our blood.

As a golfer, my most rewarding experiences in the game have occurred while chasing golf across distant lands. Fueled by a wild desire to see more courses in new and faraway places, I remain a student of golf design for the expressed purpose of planning trips to play fulfilling golf holes. No matter the landform or varied geography, I want to see it all.

If the architects of golf keep building amazing places, I'll certainly keep lining up to see them. Me and thousands of others.

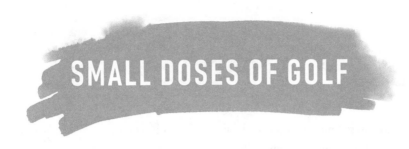

SMALL DOSES OF GOLF

You never know when or where you'll find a small slice of golf.

I've come across the game in all sorts of random places, and I always feel compelled to investigate the offering. I've found golf in city parks, dive bars, backyards, and yes: even at weddings. Golf is truly everywhere, and I've never encountered an example of the game where it did not make me smile.

If golf is available, go play it! I can't help but take the opportunity to enjoy a taste of golf when the game is offered to me. It doesn't have to be big and grand. The simple, intimate, and available will satisfy most of us.

As for me, I'm the guy who putts at a wedding, chips at a barbecue party, and jumps at the chance to make a golf shot no matter the circumstances. I'll take golf in any form I can find it. Even in small doses, the game never disappoints.

" Golf is truly everywhere "

SCORECARDS

I'd like to go out on a limb and tell you that golf scorecards are art. No two are the same, and each one tells a unique story.

I tend to prefer the simple and understated charm of a certain class of cards, but then again, I find it fun to study the busier prints that often tell a bigger story. When I think about the card from my old home course, I can't help but appreciate its representation of my favorite little town.

I'm not a big fan of clutter, but sometimes an advertisement on a scorecard will just give me a smile. Back home, the card is covered with small, rectangular business listings. Each one tells a story about someone I know. These cards are windows into the local economy and an important declaration of support for our proud golf scene.

On our card we've got auto parts, package liquor, and air conditioning repair. There are sandwich artists and a mortician, too. I can hear the heartbeat of my hometown each time I scratch down some scores there.

I keep scorecards from every course I visit, and some are clearly more attractive than others. Of course, there are many opinions about what looks good and what doesn't. My tastes in all things golf related continue to evolve, and my scorecard preferences are part of that.

Just when I think I love a minimal, pocket-sized card with the simplest of layouts, I come across some place like home where the scorecard is a way for locals to endorse and support the game. The scorecard with ads is much more than a billboard: it shows that there are people who have skin in the game.

I believe that the best art tells stories. Using my hometown scorecard as an example, there are an awful lot of stories to be told. I've come to appreciate all scorecards, because no two places are the same, and that's a great thing.

THE SOUND OF A BALL STRIKER

There is a particularly pleasing sound made when a world-class ball striker makes their way around a golf course. The crispness of contact can be heard clearly by those who observe such talent.

It's hard to articulate what exactly separates the shots of professionals from those of amateurs, but the eye and ear can tell: it's certainly visual and audible. The combination of a swift motion and effortless control make for a symphonic swing rhythm. Every golfer makes noise at impact, but the very best make music.

Watching a professional up close is like sitting in the front row for Swan Lake. Enchanting doesn't begin to adequately describe the scene. If you want to know the difference between good and great, just listen for the sound.

"the very best make music"

AMERICAN DREAMS

Golf and the American Dream go hand in hand. For starters, the game is incredibly democratic, in that the course doesn't care what your background is. The lowest score always wins, and hard work is equally rewarded.

Despite being a challenging pastime, people still flock to the game. Golf, for many people, is their pursuit of happiness. Whether it's a long walk with friends on your home course, an annual group trip to a ritzy resort, or just sipping the coldest beer at the local muni, golf is a great game for chasing and realizing dreams.

Those dreams are different for everyone who plays the game, and amazingly, many of them come true. Some people want to hit a hole in one and others want to break 100. There are those who aspire to join private clubs and others who are just in it for a hot dog at the turn. The golfing world has so many types of dreamers: the tour players, wannabes, club champions, high schoolers, range regulars, travelers, and beat-your-agers, to name a few. Then there are those who dream of living on a local course, working in the game as a professional, or heaven help me: crazy writers who like to tell stories about it all. People just can't get enough of this stuff!

Golf is both a window into your life and a portrait of your soul. In America, the game is far from perfect, but it's a reflection of all of us that play it. It's increasingly inclusive and will only become more so in the coming years. American golf is truly a melting pot. The more people bring their culture to golf, the more it evolves for the better.

Golf has long been popular in America. There are numerous reasons for this, but I like to believe it's because the game is perfectly suited as an example of our national ethos.

The opportunity to succeed isn't guaranteed, but it's more accessible and attainable than ever before. Every golfer is a dreamer of some degree, and much like America, the game should be open to anyone who wants to take a crack at it.

American golf dreams come in all forms. There's no limit to what's possible. That's America. That's golf.

ON YOUR ASS

If you aren't careful, golf will knock you on your ass. This game is tough. It's not for everyone, but it can be enjoyed by anyone willing to withstand the challenge of it all.

If you play long enough, you'll have a mix of good rounds and bad. The ups and downs of golf are reflective of our own life cycle. The important thing to remember is that even when things get sideways, you'll get back to the center again soon.

For most of us, the wayward shots will always outnumber the well struck. But if you're willing to keep swinging, the rare-but-wonderful moments will indeed find you.

That being said, it's okay to feel deflated on occasion. It's natural to think that one bad shot will result in more of them. The truth is that, despite the sinking feeling that comes with a poor result on the course, golf is still an uplifting game. It doesn't take much to lift the soul again. A few good shots and some circles or pars on the card can completely change your outlook.

The more you play, the more you'll get knocked down. The secret to mastering the game lies not in a low handicap, but instead in your personal ability to play through golf's difficulties. Like in life, the key to long-term success is always getting back up. Just keep swinging.

"Just keep swinging"

WILL THE BALL

Some golfers have an uncanny ability to will the ball into the hole. It's as if they possess a sixth sense of sorts. No matter the scenario, the ball finds its way to the cup at an inordinate rate.

Do they have some occult power used to shape outcomes? It certainly feels that way at times. Perhaps they are seers of other dimensions present in our world and can bend reality to their pleasure. Perhaps I've been watching too much tv.

To roll putts in the hole so frequently and make chip shots with regularity is a talent for which few are privileged to have: surely there are other forces at work. The player who can command the ball to turn into the cup is the hardest to defeat. They are always one unforeseeable moment away from stealing a hole and sealing their victory.

If you can look past losing to such a player, their skills are truly something to behold. Driven by a desire to win, their willpower can indeed determine their score.

RELICS

I've always been drawn to the artifacts of the past. You see, I'm a collector of sorts. I love old things. Especially when those things relate to golf.

In my home I have a room for the items I've come to possess over the years. I know the origin stories of some of them, and others I'm left to invent. Some once served a purpose in the game, and others were the reward for good play. Today, their only use is to bring me a smile when I walk by them.

Perhaps in another life I would have run a museum or sought out golf treasure like a quarter-zip-clad Indiana Jones, but I'm only a curator of my own small ensemble. My trinkets range in size and importance, but they all bring me joy. I've discovered them in attics, closets, offices, and eBay. The hickory shafted clubs, silver loving cups, cracked old golf balls, and other golf ephemera have come to me from hoarders and even some good shops. There's no special theme to my menagerie, yet when viewed together they create a visual interest that greatly appeals to this audience of one.

These old things fill my shelves and adorn my walls, giving me much to think on and appreciate as I stop in during the day. My collection helps me set a mood for reading and often inspires the words I scribble down. Most

> **these old treasures are a reflection of my inner monologue and a window into the world I try to create**

importantly, these old treasures are a reflection of my inner monologue and a window into the world I try to create. Each item is evidence of my travels and a tangible reminder of the reasons I love the game.

So much more than just antiques, I'm drawn to them like relics and ponder where to find more.

END OF THE ROUND

The 18th tee is a bittersweet place. Like the last chapter in a novel, some days I hate to see it, and on other occasions it's a welcome ending.

The last hole offers both opportunity and closure. I've come to the final hole in so many different states of mind. There have been rounds where I'm charging toward victory and need a strong finish. I've had others where I'm hanging on for dear life and just trying to get a respectable score on the board. I've limped home with my ego bruised from a bad round, and on a few occasions, I just wanted to stay out there for the incredible company or the breathtaking scenery. I've soared to closing birdies and broken down in devastating fashion. Each version begins with a club in my hand and hope in my heart.

It can be hard to focus when arriving at the last hole of the day, but in order to write a proper ending we must find a way. The finale always matters the most in our memory because it's the closing chapter. If someone argues that all shots count the same, ask them how they feel after a double bogey ending.

I always want my golf experience to end well, even if the rest of the day was poor. A solid finish makes the beer taste better after the round.

Standing on the tee box while looking down the last hole is an important moment. We've all been there and want to be there again. It's there that I try to find the confidence to close in some impressive fashion. In the end, I have to just hit the ball the best I can and take what the game gives me.

We all want a happy ending, but in golf there's no guarantee. The only way to close the game is to swing away and see what happens.

SNACK SHACK

I love a good snack shack. My golf friends can vouch for that.

The halfway house is a welcome break in the action. A quick pit stop before returning to battle the back nine.

Most are unremarkable stopovers—good for a cold beer or a candy bar but some stand out for sure. I've sampled burger dogs at Pasatiempo, scarfed grouper tacos at Streamsong, sipped Tomahawks at Timuquana, and nibbled on homemade cookies in Aiken. Some places even have the perfect takeaway items, like the chili at Bay Hill or chicken salad at Chanticleer.

Sustenance is good for the swing, and when traveling sometimes the snack shack is the best chow I can find. Not every course has one, but they should!

The key to a great turn house is to have a fun setting, personable service, and a delicious signature item. Simplicity is often rewarded in this field. People don't want fussy. Instead, just give us the tasty, easy to get, and refreshing food and drink.

Some places specialize in their eats, while others stir a great cocktail. Those who do it well will keep the customers coming back for more. In some cases, the stories of such wonderful treats will travel far and wide, creating a powerful reputation. If someone ever tells you about a snack shack they enjoyed, you best go check it out, because those accolades don't get tossed around lightly.

If that recommendation comes from a connoisseur like me, you can rest assured it's because that place has the goods.

SUNSET

My favorite spot to watch the sunset is only a few blocks away from my house. I walk there quite often to see the spectacle that occurs as the sun slips over the Southwest horizon at dusk. I take my golf clubs of course, and my family comes too. And maybe the dog, if he's well behaved.

The evening fireworks commence about a half an hour before darkness falls on the city. I like to watch the fading of the light and the parade of colors that comes with it.

We walk out onto the course from the streets of our neighborhood, through an opening in the live oaks where the maintenance team enters and exits each day. Asphalt gives way to grass, and as I step through this portal the sky begins to illuminate. It's an idyllic location to hit a few chips and putts before the nightly toddler routine takes us home.

There are two greens there snuggled closely together, for the 4th and 13th holes, where I hit shots to hone my craft. I set up shop with a shag bag and proceed to practice, while my dog watches with intrigue and my wife plays in the sand trap with our daughter.

From this spot—the highest elevation on the course—we have front row seats to a breathtaking performance. Most every night we have this magical little mesa all to ourselves. Standing there with club in hand, family at my side, and the sun sinking fast, I can easily enjoy all the things I love most in this life. I can't imagine any sunset location more perfect, and I hope to make it there for a thousand more.

THE EDGE OF SANITY

Sometimes you've got to know when to walk away. Golf will push you to the edge of sanity if you let it.

It's okay to take a break.

Anyone who knows and loves golf can tell you that this game will drive you nuts. Yips, shanks, pulls, shoves, hook, slice: there's no shortage of swing disease that can infect your game. The best medicine is often just some time away from the game.

Among the many schemes available for shooting lower scores, nothing works as well as a burning desire to play. When the game gets us down, that can be a hard passion to summon. Taking time off can help to rekindle those flames.

For the diehards it's hard to imagine taking a prolonged sabbatical from golf, but don't be afraid to try it. If you play the game long enough, you'll go through cycles of both dis-couragement and bliss. As Shivas Irons suggested, golf is a game for the in-between times. It's in those periods of rest, when we halt our constant state of searching, that we can often find our center again. We walk away so that we can soon come running back.

" Taking time off can help to rekindle those flames "

A DIRTY RIGHT TOE

The importance of footwork in a golf swing can't be overstated. Everything begins with a strong and properly aligned base.

The stance is the foundation for movement. Lose your footwork, and you'll lose your swing.

When things go awry in my game, it's probably because my alignment is off. I know this, and yet instead of making a corrective adjustment with my feet, I usually try everything else first. Golfers are quick to want to make other changes, and for some strange reason our feet are usually the last thing we think of.

Gramps always told me that the best way to spot a good player is to look for a dirty right toe. If properly aligned and swinging through to the target, the good player's right toe should be pointed down and twisting through the soil like a corkscrew. This move is meant to serve as a fulcrum for the finish of a golf swing.

As Gramps would say, "the dirt on the big toe means you finished the swing." The easiest way to fix my footwork is to think of that big right toe. That small digit is indeed the key to balance.

Power, finesse, and smoothness of the swing are all grounded by one common factor: footwork. It's high time this segment of the swing got more attention. We should all strive to dirty our right toes and be better golfers.

LEARNING THE GAME

Golf is not learned the same by everyone. For some, the game is intuitive.

Most who try to learn golf look foolish, but there are some who find their swing straight from the start. Incredibly, they just know how to do it.

Anyone who is beginning to learn will be deficient in the mechanical details, yet there are certain new-to-the-game golfers who seem to have a head start. How can this be?

Golf skill is not a genetic trait, and for something so difficult, it's hard to imagine anyone could just have a knack for it. It happens, though. Golf offers guarantees to no one, but there are some who appear to possess a gift—a blessing if you will—that allows them to improve at a faster rate.

Some may be starting ahead of the game, but it's still up to them to put in the work needed to build on the generosity they were offered by the golf gods. Therein lies the rub: the difference between the wasted and the realized comes down to drive and desire.

It doesn't matter where the golfer begins their journey. What matters is that they stay on it. That only happens with a foundation built around a deep personal love for the game.

A little natural ability and some good old-fashioned hard work can take a golfer quite a long way, but in the end, a passion for the game will be what keeps them in it.

"the difference between the wasted and the realized comes down to drive and desire"

DAYLIGHT SAVINGS

How wonderful it is to see the return of longer days and golf after work. Daylight Savings Time is a savior for golfers who must punch the clock from nine to five.

Empty courses turn lively again after the whistle blows. We rejoice as the sun stays out long past its bedtime. The budding beauty of spring is a siren to golfers everywhere. Clubs are dusted off and friendships are rekindled. The welcomed seasonal warming sets the stage for busy tee sheets and crowded grill rooms.

After a sleepy winter, working on assignments and counting the hours, we gladly greet the opportunity to put our duties aside for a while and participate in our favorite pastime. With long to-do lists at both work and home, it's easy to understand why everyday golfers delight in longer days and more time to unwind at the course. The golf is out there, and all we have to do is go get it.

In this new season, range sessions, short loops, and nine-hole leagues sprout up like wildflowers. For seven months the evenings are once again made for golf, and each day offers the opportunity to make a few swings before sundown. This is golf season, and aren't we glad it's back.

GOLF PRAYER

Golfers pray for many different things. When playing well, we pray for more chances to tee it up. When our game is poor, we pray for improved fortunes. On cold days our prayers are for sunshine, and on hot afternoons we hope for shade. When behind in a match, we pray for birdies. If holding onto a lead, we just ask for pars. Clinching the tees in our pocket like a rosary, we pray over putts we need to drop and chips we want to see settle close.

From bended knee, golfers pray to get up and down from bunkers. We plead to drive the pond, lake, stream, and cove. We pray for the clouds to part and the rain to stop. Like desperate souls seeking salvation, we pine for vacations and the chance to escape reality on far-flung courses.

Over a lifetime, golfers pray for Masters tickets and Old Course tee times. Prayers for inner peace and steady strokes are made under the pressure of competition. Recovery shots require a bit of prayer, too. We beg for the chance to play again tomorrow and again the day after that. Prayers are sent up to the heavens for all matters of the game.

Prayers on the course are both quiet and pronounced. They can be shouted and will certainly be whispered. Prayer on the course may seem out of line, but for many this spiritual game gives the golfer a chance to connect not only with nature but with a higher being.

Does it help to pray in golf? That's up to each of us to say, but in the end, if you want to know the truth about the power or prayer in golf, only God can answer your call.

MEDITATION

Take a deep breath. Hold it in for a few extra seconds. Exhale and find your center. Stress and anxiety may be all around you, but that doesn't mean you can't arrive at a state of personal peace.

Golf is good for this. A long walk can awaken the soul, especially on the golf course. The repetitive nature of the game has the ability to distract from the pressures of everyday life. There is hope for anyone who is unafraid to become lost in the process of playing golf.

Golf is powerful in many ways, most of all because it helps to forget about the pervasive problems that would otherwise dominate your thoughts. We all need to meditate, and this beloved pastime is a way of doing that.

Golf is a means for quieting the mind. Let the game lead you there. Take a deep breath, hold it in, and slowly exhale. Everything else is just the space between swings.

"Let the game lead you there"

GOLF'S BEST FRIEND

There's no better place to walk the dog than on the golf course. We all want to stretch our legs: imagine if you had four of them!

The golf course is an ideal place for enjoying nature, getting some sunshine, and finding composure. Remember how much a walk on the course can help improve your mood. The same can be said for our canine friends.

If you're heading to the course these days, take the dog with you if you can. A happy dog is one of the great joys in life. If the golf course brings you joy, it's easy to see how it can do the same for your dog. Abide by the rules, show common courtesy, and train your pup up well. You'll both be glad to have more golf in your lives.

WHAT WE SEARCH FOR

What are we searching for? The golfer is on a never-ending quest for answers. We keep looking, but each time we seem close, the maze just leads us off course.

Sometimes this game feels like a permanent purgatory. No way to win, and no way out. We wander from round to round and place to place hoping to find the center, but most times we just end up down another endless passage.

But the quest is not without joy. There are moments along the way that justify our continued pursuit. The shots, putts, scores, and rounds that empower our curiosity are more than enough to overlook the bad bounces, lip-outs, lost bets, and shanks that populate the time in between. We press on with no understanding of why, because if we can just find the next glorious encounter, then perhaps it will lead us to the golfing promised land.

We play on in search of those instances that defy logic and rules. The search isn't for the meaning of golf, it's for a better understanding of our place in the game.

" perhaps it will lead us to the golfing promised land "

LETTING GO

We all carry the weight of everyday emotions squarely on our shoulders. However, golf can allow us to forget that pressure from time to time.

We worry about our jobs, family, and other heavy matters, but those who play golf can find relief in the game. Golf can transport us. It can lift our hopes.

Golf is a way to disperse the weight we carry. Every so often, through golf we can find a higher plane of thinking. Relaxed and without worries, this is the desired mentality.

It's amazing to watch when someone is playing with that capacity. It's life changing when it happens to us. The hardest thing to shake off in this existence is the dense weight of our worrisome world. Golf is a means for overcoming these negative forces, though. If you can let go—even for a little while—great things will come.

FOUR-BALL

Competitive golf can be a real grind. It helps to have a partner who can help get you through it. That's why as I get older, I mostly prefer to play in four-ball tournaments.

I love the feeling of playing golf as a team. There are always ups and downs during these events, and they often become a battle. But it's so much fun to draft off one another and share in the highlights of a tense round.

Sometimes everything clicks and scoring is a breeze. Then there are days where it gets tough to keep the bogeys off the card. No matter the mood, the only way to win is if you play as partners.

Running down birdies and securing necessary pars turns into quite the sport. Things can get interesting when one player gets on a hot streak, or even when one goes cold. Because of that reality, four-ball events bring out all sorts of emotions.

What's needed is balance. Both players have to try and meet the other half way. When it all comes together, great things can happen.

After the tournament ends and I sit down to share drinks and stories, it's much more enjoyable to have a partner there to relive it all. Golf may be mostly an individual game, but it's a better time when you're part of a team.

HOPE

Hope is not just a feeling: it's a life force. It's why we get out of bed in the morning and certainly why we head to the first tee time and time again. Hope is an essential part of golf.

We hope to play well, just like we hope to have rich and fulfilling lives. Every comparison between golf and life is built off a foundation of hope. To be a golfer, one must be filled with belief.

Hope is why we go for the green from a difficult lie, despite the pond in our way. It's how we stir just enough courage to take on the tucked pin. Hope is a reason to cut the corner and fuel for the choice to try a desperate shot against long odds. It's why we like to stand over the must-make putt. It's why we give every swing our best effort. If we have hope, we have everything.

The game of golf may have been devised as a simple pastime, but in truth it has always been a complicated expression of hope. As long as there is golf, there will always be hope in the world.

Golfers are guardians of hope. We are the believers in the impossible and witnesses to miracles. The dream lives in us, and we are the reason it remains tied so closely to our game. While we play, we hope.

TRY LESS, MAKE MORE

The harder you try to make a putt, the less likely it'll go in. The best putters see a line and a speed, and then simply roll it with feeling. It may sound counter-intuitive, but to be a player who makes more putts, you need to turn the effort down.

Success on the greens starts with an understanding that some putts will go in and some won't. This frees the mind to think less and feel more. It also takes the pressure off.

A carefree putt will always have a greater chance of being holed. If you can develop a system for rolling the ball toward your target and accept whatever happens, then you'll start to see more putts drop. Try less, make more.

BACKYARD GOLF

Every golfer should have a backyard hole. All you need is a little pitch shot in order to have a place to work on your game.

For me, my backyard golf hole is a place to find serenity and balance. Measuring a whopping 25 yards long, the hole I created is one that helps me find a little sanity during difficult times.

Great for a golf break while working from home, my backyard hole has generated some huge upside for my mental health. Having a place to go, and walk, and make some swings matters greatly when facing stress.

Additionally, I've found the hole in our yard to be a great addition for cocktail parties, family dinners, and toddler physical education. My backyard hole has many design flaws, but when I need a few quick swings and space to do some thinking, it certainly gets the job done.

CAMARADERIE

There is no substitute for the camaraderie that comes from a crowd of golfers. A mixture of both strangers and friends can easily mingle when they all share a common love for the game.

There is a rising chatter that rings through those gathered together; a sign of excitement no doubt. Laughter, shouting, and other loud levels of communal conversation are a hallmark of golf gatherings. We enjoy libations and share tall tales with great enthusiasm.

For golfers, having fun is rather contagious. Even a bad round will be made better through the nearness of friends and kindred spirits. There are a great many reasons to play golf, but among the best are the moments spent with a large crowd of players who share a passion for the game.

HICKORY CLUBS

Trying to hit a hickory-shafted 2 iron sounds fun until you try it. I take that back ... I've never really hit any 2 iron very well. Perhaps vintage clubs just make you look sillier.

It's hard to say why anyone would want to use equipment from a bygone era, and yet there are droves of us who enjoy such antiquated activities. I ponder this question each time I send a hosel rocket off the end of that wood-handled 2 iron of mine. Maybe it's a form of self-mutilation, cutting one's pride instead of body parts.

I can attest to the effectiveness of shanky swings with hickory clubs, when trying to keep one's ego in check. I keep a bag of these peculiar sticks hanging on my garage wall, in my golf club menagerie. I don't pull them out too terribly often, but there's no better way to find out how your new swing thought is holding up than to mishit these things for a few holes.

With a hickory-shafted club, a solid swing will send shockwaves through my central nervous system, a clearly identifiable sign that something in my swing is working as good as it should. A few well-struck shots with these time-capsule clubs can only be the result of a specific rhythm.

Hickories are not made to show your power. Instead, they showcase a softer set of skills. Hickories are a way to find the face again. They're a means for making amends when a swing falls out of whack.

Hickories are a stripped-down version of golf, and they'll damn sure undress the flaws of those who swing them. I don't want to play the hickory game every day, but it's a fine way to see where my swing stands while having a chuckle at the madness of this game.

THE ZONE

Some days my game clicks into place, and the golf just makes sense again. Hell, when I hit it on the screws for 18 holes, the whole world makes sense. Golf can seem so simple.

It's funny how golf can make even the strangest of times more joyous. A good, long walk and some crisp ball striking is a great prescription for when life gets crazy. In trying times, it's good to get lost in something you love.

"In trying times, it's good to get lost in something you love"

GOLF EVANGELISM

Golf is one of life's great and simple pleasures. We tend to over-complicate the game, but in reality, it remains something that can be played almost anywhere and by anyone. Even the youngest of children can understand the concept of hitting a ball, with a stick, into a hole.

Golf can be played in fields, forests, towns, and parks. Yes, golf lives in country clubs, but it also thrives in backyards, on farms, in offices, and even city streets. Golf has many layers, and the game is certainly not easy, but it's also one that can be enjoyed in small doses and tight spaces. There are very few guidelines for what constitutes a golf hole. Golf is everywhere!

There are even fewer qualifications for who is a golfer. We all are! The game should be played across every community and enjoyed for its ability to encourage fellowship and the exploration of the great outdoors. All we need for golf is a club and a ball, and some agreed-upon target to pursue. This is a simple game, and in troubled times we need it in every form and anywhere we can get it.

Go forth and golf. Swing, walk, and repeat. Make the game live where you do, and share it with others. Show them the way that someone once showed you. We need golf, and golf needs its evangelists. Let's play, shall we? Golf can't wait. Find the game and share it, wherever you may be.

PICK UP THE TEE

Don't you just love it when you stripe one?

The feeling of proper execution is immediately recognizable. You watch the first few seconds of your shot and confirm it's not wavering. It's that "pick up the tee" sensation that never gets old. The result of a well-struck shot flying down the target path is beautiful to behold.

"They're fuel for the golfer's soul"

Those are the shots that remind us we can indeed play to the best of our abilities. What a feeling to know how the shot will turn out long before the ball comes down. These are the swings we come back for, the ones we can't get enough of. They're fuel for the golfer's soul.

BODY LANGUAGE

Even body languages have different dialects.

There isn't a golfer alive who doesn't become a contortionist when trying to influence the result of their shots. Back bends, raised arms, forward leans, and leg kicks are all common moves. There are knee drops, quick spins, club sweeps, and table tops, too.

Golfers believe that such voodoo can actually help the outcomes of a swing, long after the ball left the clubface, and they may just be right. With so many different body types in the game, the involuntary wriggling which occurs after contact is as varied as the menu at Baskin Robbins.

There are lots of choice words reserved for a golf ball flying through the air, but the most interesting language comes from the flailing of limbs and twisting of the torso. How a golfer reacts to a golf shot says something about them. While words are important, it's the non-verbal elements that often say more.

Such moves are evidence of belief and expressions of hope. They show that deep inside we trust in the notion that the ball may just break in the cup or bounce the right way if we can only wish it so. It's unlikely that the wringing of one's body can aid in the final verdict of a golf shot, but if it didn't have some effect, then why do so many experience the same phenomenon?

The only answer must be that if one believes in a superstition, then it must at least be real to them. That's good enough for most of us.

A GOOD CADDIE

A good caddie can make a world of difference in golf. It's hard to overestimate the value of a seasoned looper when playing a challenging course for the first time. This is particularly true in places which might be described as once-in-a-lifetime experiences.

With a golfer likely having only one chance to play such a place, the caddie's advice is often essential to good scoring and making happy memories. The best caddies take pride in this and place a premium on helping their players discover some good shots. For a great caddie, though, the job is so much more than gunning yardages and reading putts.

The real work of a caddie is manufacturing confidence in a golfer. Playing a new course is hard enough, but when you factor in the added pressure of likely never returning there, it can be difficult to execute good golf. However, with the sage guidance of a trustworthy caddie, a player can rise above their fear and nerves to author a round they can be proud of.

Caddies are far more than carriers of golf clubs. They're companions and teachers, shepherds and sherpas, field guides and gurus, all wrapped into one package. Results may vary with the looper on hand, but it won't take long to know when you have a great one on the bag. They will be the ones building up your confidence before you even make the first tee. If the course you are playing has caddies available, take one. More times than not, you'll be damn well glad you did.

TIGHT SPOTS

Golf will put you in some tight spots. So will life, of course. It's easy to get swept up in the pressures of it all.

At our best, we can manage through the most difficult jams by having a strong resolve to persevere. The way we get back on track is to first get out of trouble. We can only do this one swing at a time. As the saying goes, take your medicine.

Sometimes it takes everything we have to keep plodding along while we wait for better results. The seasoned golfer frets not, for there's always hope for those who can just keep swinging. Head down, calmly focused, and committed to a plan of action: that's the epitaph every golfer should aspire to. Those who press on hold the power to recover.

The shots we make when blown off course are often the ones that define us. If a golfer can believe in pushing forward from a problem, then there's always a chance to do something special. No matter what hazards you encounter, find a way out and carry on.

" Those who press on hold the power to recover "

THE GOLF SPOUSE

Seeing someone you love fall in love with golf is a special blessing. My wife is my best friend, and over the course of our relationship she has enjoyed spending time with me through golf.

Never much for playing herself, she has joined me for many afternoons as I chase down my golf obsession. She has some clubs that I assembled a few years ago, but they've only been out for a handful of rounds as she tags along by my side. But, as golf is prone to do, the game may finally be pulling her in.

During her first ever nine-hole outing, Sarah made a series of well-struck shots, and her putting stroke was quite steady. Sarah's swing was fast to improve through the round, which gave her a rising confidence: a credit to her coordination and competitive nature, no doubt.

Even with me as her stand-in golf coach, she was turning out some highly impressive beginner swings. The best among them came on a short par three, the 6th hole at our home course. That's where she hit unquestionably the best shot of her life: a driver to the front fringe, and then proceeded to make a two-putt par. The par putt she made was nearly 10 feet!

As the ball rattled the flagstick and dropped in the hole, I saw in her the look of a brand-new golf addict. The joy in her expression and genuine nature of her excitement made for one of the great moments in my golfing life. How refreshing to see someone record their first par!

That person being my beloved wife gave me as unique a euphoria as I have experienced in golf. In her reaction I saw the woman I love, and the game I love to play, both at their very best. What more could a golfer and spouse ask for?

Like all beginners, she's still got lots to learn. I have a feeling that her early success in the game may soon lead to frustration and torment, but for now, all she has is a new love for golf. Seeing Sarah play with such grace shouldn't come as a surprise to me, but it did. After seeing her jubilation first hand, I have a sense that she will be playing much more golf in the future. Maybe I can be her partner in this game, too.

MASTERY

No matter how young we start, there's no way to avoid the pitfalls and pains of golf. But to fail is to learn, and to learn is to grow. That's what we as golfers are truly seeking to do: grow with the game.

We hope not to repeat mistakes, and we strive to improve each day. When we are young, it's hard to appreciate the value of a few hours for golf. But as we age, we discover that the time required to learn slowly disappears. In order to stay with the game, we must find those hours again.

We need that child-like curiosity to drive us and keep us close to golf. People stay near the things they love, and that's what this game takes. If we can keep our love for the game, then there's always a chance to find our place in it.

" we must find those hours again "

THAT GUY

Every golf club has that one guy. You know him: the one who's hard to root for. Make no mistake, he's your friend. That's actually part of the problem. You are mates. Old chums. Running buddies. If you are playing on the same side, you love his smack talk and good play, but when he's on the other side—twisting the dagger with a smile—you just can't take it.

He's good. The guy is a stick. He's also a smart ass and a clown. But he's kind of your clown. Until he's not. It's not that you root against him: you just can't bring yourself to find the joy in him kicking your ass. He gets all the good breaks, makes all the putts, and has a particularly pointed way of bringing up the status of your match.

Beating him is a special pleasure. In large part due to its rare occurrence. The word insufferable comes to mind, yet you still play with him. He's a bad habit and a broken record. A rolled ankle, migraine, and toothache all rolled into one. This nagging pain of a friend is a hell of a player. He'll take your money and make you feel the loss of every cent. He will also do it with a smile, a crooked smirk that can only signal that he's won again.

Most times all you can do is laugh—or cry—or maybe just yell into your arm. Golfers like him give the game a bad name, but he also is the first guy you think of when it's time to go play. He's your golf pal and a tormenting demon. Yet still, you call him friend. Only golf can produce such strange relationships.

You might think he's a nut, but then again there you are right there with him each time. He hits the shots and talks the shit. He's also one more reason to love golf. What an enduring enigma.

TO THE NEXT TEE

Golf is a grand adventure. We take that journey one step at a time. My favorite steps are the ones that happen while walking from one hole to the next.

Sometimes those walks are lengthy, with too much time to think. The best are short strolls when the golf course tells you to stay buckled in or "don't leave the moment." There's plenty of time for reflection later.

During the round, I like walks that keep the action in front of me. Those few moments between holing a putt and taking off for the next tee are among the best in golf. Architects should be careful not to disrupt the rhythm of good play with overly distant walks between holes. Instead, a routing—and in particular the transitions—should be made to keep the player in tune with the pace of a course. That's why I enjoy such courses that allow for swift migration between holes.

Great courses feel symphonic in nature. The senses should remain activated through rising and falling emotional intensity. The most anxious moments in golf are often on the putting green and the next tee box. That's when the music of a round should be hitting the high notes. Give me the steady beat that comes from my feet leading from a made putt to the hope of a new hole.

The walk from green to tee is the mortar that holds a course together. An ideal course should appear seamless. Not a collection of golf holes, but instead a tapestry of challenges strung together beautifully across the land. The distance between greens and tees isn't always a good measure of a course, but typically it's a sign of the certain attention paid to the craft.

Golf design is landscape art, and the best practitioners spend lots of time working on what happens between holes. For those who have never considered the importance of these walks, I encourage you to look again. The transitions from one hole to the next are often some of the most revealing characteristics of a golf course.

STRANDED ON AN ISLAND

Sometimes, golf makes me feel like I'm stranded on an island. Like Tom Hanks in *Castaway*, the only thing holding my game together is a sliver of hope.

It's not that I'm lost: it's worse than that, because I know exactly where I am and there simply is nowhere to go. In those moments I know there's no boat or rescue coming to save my swing. Instead, I must find and fight my own way out.

In order to get off my island, I'll have to first choose the direction I want to paddle in. Things will most certainly get choppy along the way, but if I can dig deep, find my fundamentals again, and remain on course, then perhaps I can make it back to the swing I once knew so well.

When my game leaves me searching, it's easy to feel alone. Of course, the island is just a metaphor. Despite a feeling of loneliness, I'm usually surrounded by others who are stuck there with me in what seems like golfing purgatory.

At times my game can make me feel like I'm firmly planted on a deserted island, but the population there is actually quite large. We all stand on the shore, scanning the horizon for hope that just as golf put us in this place, the game will someday bring us home.

" the game will someday bring us home "

CHARGE ON

When things go awry, the golfer must charge on. The most important virtue for golfers is persistence. Even through the bad swings, we know we can't give in.

The golfing wilderness is no place for those who are light in character. Having a will to win is easy. Having a will to stay in the fight when you so badly want to quit is hard.

Those with the spirit to endure and get comfortable with the uncomfortable are to be admired. They are the players we all should emulate. The pathway to better performance in golf is riddled with failures. The bad swings always outnumber the great. To become a good golfer, you must be someone willing to submit to the tortures of bad rounds at a highly regular rate.

Oh, and there are demons, too. Only the most committed to the game can stagger through such living nightmares as the shanks, yips, and tops. The true golfer is in love with this game and can't be shaken.

Despite such overwhelming odds against success, these are the players who press forward. To do so means enduring more of the bad in order to get to the good. The only way through a dark passage is straight through. As daunting as that sounds, one good swing is all you need to get back on track. The hunt for another solid swing happens one step at a time. Heads up, spirits high, and focused. We will all have our fair share of bad days, maybe even more. But we go again in the morning.

THE FOUR-LEGGED
GOLF LIFE

I like to think that a dog's life is made better by golf. The same is true for the owner of course.

My dog Leon is at his best when we are making some late afternoon swings. He's a damn fine companion for such outings. Among his many attributes, it's his listening skills that I tend to be most impressed by. I talk to him quite a bit, and of all my friends he interrupts me the least.

I'm sure he's tired of hearing my old stories ... most folks are. He sticks around, though. We go way back, you see. He pretends to be interested in my opinions, and for that I'm eternally grateful. After all these years we both know our way around each other.

Leon recognizes all my bad habits—both in golf and in life—yet he passes no judgment. There is only forgiveness in the eyes of a dog. He keeps good company for me and I for him. Our long walks together for golf are among my best moments each week.

Some days I wonder if I chose him or he chose me. Either way, we've made quite the journey together. We've both aged a lot, but somehow, he's still the better looking of our duo: likely the result of stress from the many years of my poor putting.

He's a calming influence on me and a stable force in my game. I like to think he's just as into golf as I am, but in reality, he's probably just glad to be out of the house.

The course is where he runs free and wild. Leon has earned his right to walk those holes with no restraint. He minds his manners and abides by the rules, mostly. There are the occasional bunker walk-throughs; leaving footprints like the moon landing. It's a little hard to explain the concept of a hazard to him. What he does get is me. I believe he knows that the course is a special place, and I'm confident he senses why I love being out there.

Our reasons for enjoying the course may be different, but we both get to soak in it together. Each round of golf is a blessing, and a good dog only makes it better. I think we will keep at it for as long as we both can. He's my pal, he's my pet, and he fills me with pride. I'm lucky to have a dog who shares my passion for golf.

MOM'S SWING

My mom doesn't play much, but she's got one heck of a good swing. I wouldn't expect anything less from the daughter of a club pro. I can see elements of Gramps' swing in hers. The only thing she's missing is more reps.

Mom just needs to play. I admit: my wish that she would tee it up more is somewhat rooted in my own self-interest. I want my daughter to have as many role models in golf as possible. I hope she can see my wife and mom both enjoying the game. That will do far more for her interest in the sport than anything I can teach her.

I come from a golfing family, and now that it's growing, I'd like to see us all on the course more. There's something special about playing with those you love, and it's hard to imagine anything more enjoyable. When we get Mom on the course, it's a real treat. As Dad likes to say, "you need to be playing some golf!" I hope we can all be together on the course more and see Mom's swing for many years to come. I think she could even teach me a few things.

> **I want my daughter to have as many role models in golf as possible**

KINDRED SPIRITS

Golf makes for remarkable friendships. The game reminds us of our better angels and connects kindred spirits. These golf friendships come through both proximity and shared experiences.

Golfers are near one another for extended periods of time: an environment conducive to the forging of strong bonds. Despite the appearance of a silly game taking place, a much more important ritual is happening.

Golf serves as a method for uniting those who play it. When this shared pursuit is frequently repeated, our similarities become increasingly evident while our personal differences disappear. Golf is a bridge between our souls. What a noble pastime to pursue.

CONFIDENCE

Golf is a game of confidence. That feeling comes and goes with our swings and strokes. When confidence is high, anything is possible. While low, it's hard just to take the club back. It's the idealist in us that we need to cultivate, while drowning out the realist for a minute.

Confidence is how we make the ball move on command. It's how we walk a putt in from a few feet out. Confidence is tested with a drive over a hazard and a pitch from a tight lie. It's gained from good shots, but it's also necessary to hit great shots. It's every breathtaking shot you can remember hitting.

Confidence goes beyond just believing. The confident player knows they can summon their swing when needed. They know the putt is going to drop. To unlock these powers is to find a new level of playing the game. When a good player develops some confidence, they can become an unstoppable force.

Confidence isn't found but created. It takes work: self-belief is a hard emotion to achieve for so many golfers. It starts with strong fundamentals and is cemented by practicing good habits. We all have the ability to walk tall on the fairways and feel powerful on the greens. It takes reps to build confidence. That happens one swing at a time. In order to be confident, one must be willing to do that work.

A DEBT TO THE GAME

Every golfer owes a debt to the game. We pay that down by sharing the sport with others. For me, that starts with those I love the most.

My greatest joy in golf today is seeing my daughter Winnie take a swing. She laughs when she hits it well, and that's just the coolest feeling. It's hard to imagine ever getting any better moments than those from golf.

Helping someone learn the game is incredibly fulfilling. Those little lessons serve as a reminder for why we must learn to be patient in golf. Patient and passionate teachers are the key to golf spreading its reach into new generations.

We might want to teach a great swing, but first let's teach people how to have fun. We must show others the way someone once showed us. You'll never regret giving the gift of golf. It's a gift we should pay forward.

❝ Helping someone learn the game is incredibly fulfilling ❞

THE WALK WE TAKE

The walk we take in golf mirrors our journey in life. If you keep moving long enough, the game will bring you back around.

Life is cyclical like that, too. We cover great distances: moving one step at a time, but always come back to where we started. Back to square one.

Each time around, the quest is different. Some routes are easy, others are hard, but the fact that we get to go forth is far too important to forget. What we learn along the way—about ourselves and others who share the walk with us—is the real reason we play the game.

We should all take more time to appreciate the paths we find ourselves on in life and in golf. There is much to learn along the way.

THE COURSE IS CALLING

We aren't meant to live sedentary lives. We are designed to move, explore, and wander. The cages we make for ourselves do not suit the true nature of our souls.

We all have an internal compass that points to a more adventurous life. To follow it we must seek different fates from those that have been handed us. It's our destiny to return to the joyous pursuits we most desire.

We hear the call and feel compelled to venture in new and bold directions. Setting forth toward a fresh perspective, finding a different understanding for how things will be. Golf is the answer. The time to go into the game is now. The further we press forward, the closer we come to our best selves. The course is calling, and we must go.

" Golf is the answer "

LOST BALLS

I've never stopped to ponder how many golf balls I've lost in my life, but the number must be astronomical. When considering my formative years in the game, all the bad breaks through the years—misses of every form imaginable, and a few spells with the shanks—I've ditched enough dimpled orbs to fill up Shamu's swim tank. Titleist could have run a plant just on my own misfortune.

I've hunted down golf balls across all sorts of wild terrain. Balls have been lost to bushes, bridges, ponds, and snakes. They've stuck in trees, sucked in mud, slid under leaves, and disappeared in sand. I've sent shots flying over roads, careening off homes, bouncing off cars, and even hit my fellow human. The worst part is hearing the seconds tick away each time the search draws to an end.

There have been plenty of provisionals, too. I've walked back to tees and dropped balls all over the place. My only comfort for that misery is when I find the missing balls of some other lost soul with a golf obsession, knowing then, at least I'm not alone.

Good friends have helped me search and the best pals have pity. At some point, we all are on the same hunt.

In a few decades, I've made the deep woods and glistening lakes of my home course a urethane graveyard. This is the rite of passage for all golfers, though. Searching for balls is a part of the game.

I've got an eye for tracking down lost pellets, but they still go absent far too frequently. Good, bad, or otherwise, I'm still on the hunt. I'm in a constant state of tracking down the results of dismal swings. Incredibly, the more I play, the more balls I lose, and somehow, I just want to try the game again. What a way to recreate. There's no telling where I'll hit one next.

PLAYING NEAR THE EDGE

The edge is always closer than you think. We are all just one bad bounce away from putting a big number on the card.

The margin between lucky and doomed is razor thin. That being said, the greatest rewards are most often found near the hazards. To capture the biggest prize, we must take on these risks. Only the daring can become great.

There is no shortage of players who lay up, play smart, or aim for par. There are also many who are always willing to give it a go. No guts, no glory. Some swings turn out well, and others go astray. Most times, when the perfect shot won't come, a near miss is still good enough to stay in the game.

Even still, the highest payoff can only occur when you take on the uncertain, the low-percentage play. The only way to know what you're made of is if you shoot your shot. The worst that can happen is you wind up in the comfort of a drop zone. Or maybe that topped 3-wood turns out to be a fine layup.

Whatever happens, you hit and hope. If you want to win big, the edges are going to come into play. Go for it.

BACKYARD SWINGS

Proximity matters. My backyard golf hole—affectionately known as Camellia Field Club—is a place where I can walk out of my house and immediately take some swings. Although the hole is only 30 yards long, it still allows for meaningful practice.

Despite living only a few blocks from my home course, this little hole is often the only golf I can get in a given day. This short pitch shot gives me just enough of the game to wet my whistle. It's an appetizer of sorts.

I find myself there in the early morning with a hot cup of coffee, on my lunch breaks after a quick bite to eat, or even late at night with a good glass of wine. This golf hole pairs well with just about anything.

I take pride in its presentation and can't help but enjoy the upkeep. Everything about my backyard golf hole is a reflection of its builder. It's my own private course, and I love spending time there.

In that grassy space I enjoy being with my family too—we play, laugh, and enjoy each other's company. It's where I'm teaching my daughter the basics of golf. When we first constructed the area, there was no way to know how much it would someday mean to us.

While the whole world has been staying at home, I've been able to enjoy some golf right in my backyard. That's my kind of family time, and I wouldn't trade that for anything. Right outside of my door, there's just enough golf to scratch my daily itch for the game. It's not a perfect place, but it's all mine.

Right now, I'm making lots of memories there. It's both an escape and a shrine. An interlude if you will: further proof that golf can be played wherever I need it most.

NEVER ALONE

No golfer ever walks alone. For we—the players of this game—are all linked by common bonds.

Golf instills a certain shared voice in us all. We are always surrounded by those who share in our obsession. Even when playing alone, we can rest assured that there are others doing the same. This is a comforting notion.

Our breed is surely unique. We are the endless searchers who seek out answers that don't exist, a brethren of restless souls. No matter where we are, how we play, or who we go with, golf remains the tie that binds us. We may walk without partners on occasion, but we are most certainly never alone.

"golf remains the tie that binds us"

GRAMPS' SECRET

My grandfather has always said the secret to life is "a hard day's work, a loving wife, and a happy child."

After a productive day, and time with my family on the golf course, I find that his words are the greatest truth I've ever known.

LATE SPRING

Some of the prettiest daylight of the golfing year is found during the last gasp of spring. As the hours begin to stretch long into the evening and the hands on the clock seem to halt, the sun hangs on longer than it should, and brilliant colors fill the sky.

If you are permitted in this season to stay on the course past supper time, you'll find pictures that seem like they are painted by God. These radiant scenes are presented on the horizon as your reward for pressing on past dusk.

Whatever price you must pay to witness the magic of these golden hours is worth it. These last and fleeting moments of the day are when golf is most worth playing.

BARE BONES GOLF

When you leave the frills behind, golf is just a walk through a field. Certain meadows offer great insights into this truth.

Golf is found in all sorts of places, and the game reveals itself in many forms. The best way to learn what matters most in golf is to play on a simple course, where the bells and whistles don't exist. It doesn't take much to realize that all we really need is some open space, our true swing, and a few good mates to have a match. All the rest is just for show.

UNDER CONTROL

Golf is recreation for the body and mind. It's a walk about, a chess match, a sporting pursuit.

In this game we compete against nature, the course, close friends, and most certainly ourselves. There is no greater exercise for the spirit.

The challenges of golf bring all our senses into play. We must use both our mental and physical attributes to overcome the difficulties of each shot.

The good golf swing is the result of clear thinking and efficient movements. To perform at a high level, we must control our thoughts and our abilities. This control requires regular and diligent practice. Most importantly, it requires that we play as much as possible. The more we give to the game, the more it gives to us.

OUR PERSONAL RESOLVE

Every journey into golf is different. We all begin this game in different places, and it takes us in unpredictable directions. Our hope is that while we discover our swing and learn the ways of the sport, there will be successful scoring along the way. We soon find out that's not the real quest, though.

What really pulls us in and keeps us hooked for life is the pursuit of something much more important: we go into golf to find a new side of ourselves. The game reveals unexplored layers of our soul and presents our character center stage. We go through madness in order to find a particular type of peace. You often can't find calm until you face the struggle. The path we take to get there leaves us forever changed.

Golf alters our perception of life and strengthens the foundation of our personal resolve. The further we fall for the game, the better we become. Golf improves our existence in full.

> The further we fall for the game, the better we become

PARTNERS

Some golf partners just go together like peas and carrots. Despite the occasional cat fight, they just know how to make it work. You probably have some such duo at your course.

They hoot and holler when times are good, slapping fives, bumping knuckles, and pumping fists along the way. If things get a little hairy, they probably press each other pretty hard. They make jokes, talk smack, and poke fun at opponents. Even though they can struggle individually, one of them always seems to step up when needed. These guys will brother-in-law a scorecard all day long. They are a pair in every sense of the word. Ham & eggs, Laurel & Hardy, ketchup & mustard: you get the drift.

Teams like these don't come around every day, but when they do, success seems to linger. Average alone, outstanding together. That's what partnerships do. If you find a good mate for your matches, ride them till you get bucked.

NEVER GIVE AN INCH

Golfers will gamble on almost anything, especially among close associates. From a simple Nassau to a twisted game of Wolf, there's no shortage of ways to wager in this sport.

There is a certain thrill to chasing down the money from another person's wallet, and golfers are quite creative in their schemes. From extra holes to the putting green, the betting isn't over until everyone feels alive.

When pride is on the line, the stakes are even higher. Bragging rights and dollar bills aren't so easily won. There is always another press to be had, and if you want to win, it's best to be the player who never gives an inch.

THE HOLE OUT

Of all the things in golf that make me ecstatic, nothing sends me into an extended state of bliss like holing out from the fairway.

It doesn't happen often, and it certainly makes no sense, but this rare occurrence simply makes my soul sing.

An eagle of this variety allows my spirit to soar. Golf will knock you down hard and frequently. It's all worth it though, when the game gives you a brief moment of total joy.

The feeling of seeing a ball fly to the target with the exact purpose of a particular swing, and then disappear into the cup, is beyond compare. It's the kind of excitement that keeps me coming back, the sort of moment which makes the game worthwhile.

Hope, finally, rewarded again.

" It's the kind of excitement that keeps me coming back "

I PREFER TO WALK

I've never been a big fan of riding in a golf cart. Although they serve some purpose, I believe that the experience of playing golf is diminished when riding. I've had many fun days in carts and have made plenty of memories while riding around the course, but it's not my preferred method of play.

Carts are great for a few holes with friends and family, they are nice to have when weather threatens to disrupt, and on some courses, they are simply necessary to get around an unwalkable terrain. I'm not a zealot when it comes to opposing their use ... sometimes that's just the game.

I take a ride here and there, but I generally avoid the practice. When I walk, I see more, hear more, and enjoy more of what makes golf such a splendid outdoor pursuit. Carts disconnect me from all the things I enjoy most about golf. They even make it hard to talk to my playing companions.

In a cart, a round of golf feels very choppy. Stop and go, in and out, over and around. I like things to be a bit more leisurely than that.

Most places push golfers into carts for financial reasons, and that model doesn't make much sense to me. I really don't want to pay to be rushed around in a vehicle. For others, that's the way they like the game, and that's okay: to each their own.

A golf cart is useful, but I wouldn't recommend making it part of a golfing lifestyle. It's okay to take a ride now and then, but I've always found a walk to be more fulfilling.

A PLAYABLE PUZZLE

Every golf hole is a unique challenge. They are puzzles that the player must solve.

There are multiple factors to consider when formulating a strategy: distance, wind, pin position, hazard placement, tree trouble, and the state of one's game, to name a few. Each plan of attack is based on the details of the hole and the strengths of the player. There are but a few moments available to decide how you should proceed.

This game is about the choices that only golfers can make for themselves. Whatever is done should be done in confidence. Believing that you made the right choice is the only way to make it true. After all, there's more than one way to solve these puzzles.

READING GREENS

There is an art to reading greens. Some people seem to have a gift, while others clearly do not. There are elements of this skill set that can be taught, but mostly the talent can only be acquired through a lifetime of trial and error.

To become a good green reader, you first have to miss thousands of putts. That's what it takes to see what others cannot. There are elements of golf we simply must develop on our own. Eyesight and vision. Feel and touch. You must be able to see the line and a speed, together.

Only the quiet mind can consider these factors and take full advantage. We must be peaceful and open minded to see a putt. We must feel with our feet, but also with our eyes. The line will reveal itself to those who put their time into the game. Roll more putts than the others. Remembering that the less we try, the more we will see.

the less we try, the more we will see

BEAUTIFUL SURROUNDINGS

It's easy to get caught up in the gorgeous scenery of golf. The spoils of the game are all around us.

There is hardly a landform on earth that has yet to have a golf course laid upon it. Our game is an invitation to witness the wide variety of our world.

Golf takes place in nature, and those of us who spend our time there can only pause in appreciation of what we get to witness. We are fortunate souls to be blessed with access to such stunning beauty. It's a privilege we can never overlook.

What we take for granted we are surely bound to lose. Treasure every moment, and don't lose sight of how lucky you are to enjoy such splendid rewards from a sporting pursuit.

GOOD GOLF

The greatest thing about playing good golf is how quickly it makes us forget about our bad golf.

Sometimes when my swing gets in sync and the putter gets hot, I can start to believe that I'm the best player in town. I know that isn't true, because on other occasions I get the vicious shanks, chili-dip pitch shots, and three-putt from 10 feet. The best days are when all those demons fade into the rearview, and the only thing I can see are birdies.

Golf like that makes me feel alive. It lifts my hopes and inspires me to play on forever. I'd like to have more of those rounds.

BAD LIES

We aren't defined by our bad lies, but they do shape us. Despite the misses that lead us to unfortunate positions, the real story is how we recover.

Even in the most desperate of scenarios, it's our ability to look onward toward the goal that matters most. Bad lies happen to everyone. We should view the detours made necessary by certain predicaments as simply just part of the journey.

Bad lies happen to everyone

The difficult lies and desperate stances are what make our stories interesting. Without the occasional rise in tension, this wouldn't be much of a game. It's the drama of failure and the subsequent hope for redemption that makes golf great. What a lesson for life as well.

THE PERFECT SHOT

We all know the feeling that comes with hitting a perfect shot. The subtle ringing of the nerve endings begins in your fingertips and quickly makes its way into the hands before climbing up your arms into your chest, and then up through your heart before dispersing across the entire body. Most importantly, you can feel it in your soul.

That's why we play.

All the toil and trouble of learning this silly game—and the work required to maintain some semblance of skill—is aimed at the hope that we might hit that one shot to make it all worthwhile. Amazingly, the game gives us just enough of these strikes to keep us at it. It's all a twisted trick, though.

Finding the seldom-attained perfect shot only makes our cravings for the next one worse. We dig deeper and deeper into this hole until the light of day is gone. We are all part of a dark free fall into the golfing abyss.

But there are the occasional interludes that can help us regain our footing and climb back into the light. It only takes one swing to get in the game again. One strike. One perfect shot. Should we find it we will discover enough fuel to power our resurgence and fall back in love once more.

We all want those small moments of wonder when we can recapture the feeling of synchronicity among all our moving parts. This is our quest: the search for what's largely unattainable, yet widely possible on any given swing. It's the life and death of a golfer: the never-ending hunt for the unforgettable. Such is the pursuit for our fleeting feelings of perfection.

EMERGENCY NINE

Shall we play again? Once the morning bets are settled and lunch has been served, it's time to go back out for more golf. An emergency nine is a great way to squeeze the most out of a carefree day.

This tee time is generally reserved for the most depraved players, though: those without commitments. Cocktails may be a common pairing here, too. The game gets a bit more loose for the second go-round.

There can still be money on the line, but nobody is grinding for bogeys. You make your hay with birdies here. Swing easy and play hard. We go until we give out.

" Swing easy and play hard "

SUMMER GOLF SEASON

Summertime is synonymous with golf. Long days and high temperatures set the scene for play.

This season is a celebration of the game. All across America, golfers take to the course en masse. Here the quest for low scores and fellowship take place under a sizzling sun. The smell of sunscreen and the sensation of sweat beading on our brows is a welcome sign.

For nearly four months, golf is one of the most pressing items on the agenda. Tournaments, cookouts, laughter, and joyous moments arrive. The heat of summer turns on, and the parking lots are full. Wide-brim hats, sunblock, and bright colors populate fairways. Cold beers disappear at an alarming rate, and the water coolers always run low. The insects are humming their familiar soundtrack, and it even sounds hot. Shade is in high demand, triggering memories of a misspent youth. Between dodging rain clouds and looking for the beverage cart, players are chasing down birdies in force. Swings are served with hot dogs and a side of nostalgia. Golfers' tans return to legs, arms, and watchbands, and a playful mood settles in again.

In summer, golf is in season once more.

PRACTICE

Practice makes perfect. One of the great things about having a child is teaching them the power of good habits. A regular routine helps them to learn each day. The funny thing is, in building some repetition into my daughter's days, I've fooled around and improved my own habits.

Most evenings we walk down to the golf course as a family and spend some time banging balls around. We work on her game for a bit, and when her attention turns to building sandcastles in the bunker, I get to work on mine. Meanwhile her mom is doing lunges down the fairway or crunches on the fringe. Everyone improves a bit each day in this Revell family ritual.

More important than the practice, exercise, and play, we also get to spend some quality time together. During our routine outings, the only deadline we know of is beating the fading daylight home for dinner. That's a habit I'd like to hold on to. No matter where all this practice leads, we've already found our idea of perfect.

RAIN DELAYS

Rain delays aren't always so bad. The best ones are usually when golf doesn't stand a chance. A few friends, some cold beers, and nowhere else to go makes for good conversation. It's easy to get sucked in and often hard to leave.

The soothing sounds of summer echo through the trees, a metronome for the seasoned front-porch storytellers. The steady pounding storm mixes well with the laughter and exclamation of stranded golfers. Doctored stories and other banter travel across tables, while desperate players stare up at the sky and wonder, "is this the heavy stuff?"

Hope for golf fades with every roll of thunder. With each passing drink, the need to resume play drifts further away: disappearing like stormwater down the parking lot. Instead of a few extra holes, it's another story or a couple jokes that makes us late for dinner. If golf is going to be canceled, there are certainly worse ways to do it.

BLIND SHOTS

I love the thrill of a blind shot. Such holes require us to trust our instincts and play without seeing the target. They create a bit of anxiety and suspense in the golfer.

It's hard to know what result you'll find over the next hill, but that reality breeds excitement. It takes great confidence to choose a line and send the ball out of sight. Hope plays a role, too.

Cresting the knoll to discover a desirable finish is one of golf's great and simple pleasures. It teaches us that having faith is often better than knowing.

" It's hard to know what result you'll find over the next hill "

ONE TRUE LINE

Every putt has one true line, the perfect union between slope and speed. The ideal pairing is highest possible break point and the slowest pace that still reaches the hole.

To roll the ball on this trajectory is the surest method to make more putts. When these factors are in play, the hole is seemingly larger. There is also an increased likelihood for luck. It's a method for those who like to play the odds.

It's a fine way to win matches and pester your pals. Being a great putter is a damn good reputation to have.

RHYTHM OF A WINNER

There is a certain rhythm that accompanies a winning mindset. A cadence, if you will. The best competitors are able to slow the world down around them. With a clear, focused mind, the body can perform at incredible levels.

When you find your center, you can unlock your highest potential. Calmness breeds great success. This peace comes through focus. Nowhere is this more evident than in golf.

THE LABORATORY

Golf has given me so much in my life. The most important of these gifts has been time. Time for reflection. Time for consideration. Time to contemplate this world and my small place in it.

In the quiet moments I've been gifted through golf, I think about the things I've done right and the things I've done wrong. I wonder which of my lived experiences have shaped those outcomes. During the day I try to listen to others, and later in the evening while on the course, I aim to listen to my conscience.

The golf course is where I sort things out. It's where I talk to friends about life and speak with God about what comes after it. It's how I reconcile my actions with my beliefs, both of which are changed by what I find in myself while playing this game. I seek out time for golf for many reasons, but above all else, it's so that I can find ways to be a better person.

We all need places to do this kind of work. Especially when there's so much room for improvement. For me, golf is that.

above all else, it's so that I can find ways to be a better person

With each step, swing, chip, and putt, I'm working on so much more than my game. The man that leaves the course is never the same as the one who arrived just a few hours earlier. It's where I build the change I want to see in my life. Golf is a laboratory for my soul.

PITCHING OUT

Every golf shot requires concentration, but the pitch-out deserves a particularly high level of focus. There may be no more important shot than the one which gets a golfer back on course.

Hitting fairways and greens is the key to low-scoring days, but it's the recovery from a missed shot that often keeps a good round going. A well-earned par or a salvaged bogey are sometimes the most impressive numbers on the scorecard. That nine-foot putt you hole for an unlikely save always feels better than a routine two-putt for par.

Many players are quick to give up when faced with an adverse situation, yet those with the strongest wills savor the moment and view it as an opportunity. They know that it only takes one well-judged, fortunate shot to bounce back. That's why they stay committed. The winning golfer is resilient. The winning golfer punches out.

GOLF DEGENERATE

I'm a golf degenerate. This game has a twisted hook in me.

My love for golf started when I was young, went into hibernation for a few years, then came back with a vengeance. Since then, it hasn't let go. It's an addiction in every sense of the word.

I need golf in my days like I need oxygen. I'm not just talking about playing either: everything about the game is deserving of careful study, and I'm an eager student with my hand up in the front row.

Golf is an adventure, and I'm damn sure of it. I want to go off the beaten paths, down dead-end roads, and anywhere else that may have an interesting slice of golf culture laying around.

Of course, that presents many challenges. Every time I think that my golfing journey may be running out of time, the game finds a way to draw me back in. That's the thing about golf: I can't quit the game and it can't seem to quit me.

Golf has led me all over the map, literally and figuratively, and at this point I say yes to the game in order to see where it takes me next.

Please don't read this and think that I suffer from some sort of troublesome golfing affliction. It's the opposite. I'm happy to be in this deep on something so complex.

Golf has layers, depth, and tangled webs of dynamism. I want to plunge into its chasms and get lost in the inconclusive nature of the game. That's the space I aim to carve for myself in golf.

I know that there are no certain answers in this game, but that won't derail my quest to seek them out. It's all one long walk to me, and I'm happy to keep putting one foot after the other. Golf is everywhere, and the best way to chase it is to swing, walk, and repeat. I love the game and in an endless number of ways it keeps on loving me back. My life is a golf story told one day at a time.

THE GREAT LANDSCAPES

No other game showcases the wonders of our world like golf does. Through playing this sport, we are afforded a front row seat to the impressive scale of nature. We are also presented a case study in how our species interacts with the environment.

Golf can take us to wondrous places: places well worth seeing. The game gives us a way to be present and observant of our surroundings. In these moments we're given as golfers, it's our duty to appreciate the great landscapes of earth. Without them we wouldn't have much of a game.

GOLF WILL GET IT DONE

Golf is always worth it. Whatever it takes to get out on the course—be it walking the dog, mowing the yard, finishing those emails, or calling clients—go ahead and do it. Work and chores are important, and when they lead to golf, it's amazing how quick they'll get done.

Golf is the best of motivations! It's the ultimate way to treat yourself. It's a carrot to entice personal productivity.

When golf is on the schedule, all sorts of things get finished on time. And with efficiency and haste!

When looking for a way to inspire action in oneself, a lingering tee time will always do the trick. Golf will get it done.

"Golf is always worth it"

OLD MAN PAR

Old Man Par is an elusive foe. He constantly reminds us of our shortcomings while taunting our sensibilities. He should not be so hard to vanquish, but he is. That's why Bobby Jones kept a keen eye on Old Man Par.

To conquer Par is a deceptively simple task. Fairways and greens are the preferable path, but there are many potholes and detours faced along the way. Those who don't respect his value are sure to pay the price for such neglect.

Old Man Par doesn't yield easily: he is the ever-consistent opponent.

A CADDIE IS YOUR FRIEND

A caddie is a guide. They can lead you around a golf course and set you up for success. They are also teachers, showing you how to play each hole to the best of your ability.

Caddies are companions too, providing conversation to keep your golfing mind at ease. The job, when performed well, is much harder than it looks.

Caddies aren't just there to carry your clubs. They are with you to bring the best out of your game while assisting as you get the most from a course. In golf, this is important work.

Being a caddie requires many skills. Patience, empathy, and congeniality are important traits, too. Every day they are witness to the highs and lows of golf. They help players move on from bad shots, while also helping make incredible memories happen. The services of a great caddie elevates the experience of a special round.

Every player can benefit from what a great caddie has to offer: better golf and a better understanding of where you play it. A caddie is your friend. Take one when you can.

NECESSARY FAITH

To some degree, every golf shot requires faith. You have to believe in order to execute. Confidence is a collection of factors: ability, calmness, and past experiences to name a few. When faced with a difficult lie or challenging carry, these are the assets you must rely upon. A swing made with conviction is one that stands a chance to deliver. In golf, faith is rewarded handsomely.

" A swing made with conviction is one that stands a chance to deliver "

A BIG SHOT

When we need to hit a big shot, we must concentrate and find our true swing. It's so easy to get caught up in the imitation of others, but that's not the proper way. Instead, a wise player will discover their strength in doing the best with what they have.

Being efficient is underrated. The tactical and strategic golfer can still out-score an inconsistent opponent. To do so, we must stay within ourselves. That's why the best swing in any moment is the one that is most repeatable.

PLAY THROUGH IT ALL

When the clouds gather and the wind rises, light-hearted golfers go home. But not the die-hards. Those truly committed to the game simply slap on their rain gear and play on.

The conditions of nature aren't an excuse to go inside. They are instead an invitation to test your skills. In golf's motherland, weather is essential to the sport: it makes for a valiant pursuit.

Varied forecasts are an opportunity to experience golfing environs in new ways. When the precipitation starts and the gusts begin to blow, those who are most in love with golf prepare to go out again. Somewhere beneath a pulled-down cap—drenched by rain and challenged by the game—lies the sly smile and warmed heart of a golfer in their element. There are no stoppages here.

A RECIPE FOR HAPPINESS

Golf is a way to be with friends for extended periods of time. In those hours spent together, we form bonds and strengthen relationships.

This game is tailored to the need we all have: to be close to one another. It gives us an opportunity to engage and better understand each other. In many cases, golf even becomes the reason for new friendships to blossom.

Golf is a gateway to meaningful companionship. The more we go into the game, the closer we become to those by our side. Whether we play on weekday evenings after work, Saturday mornings in a regular group, or on yearly trips with those we only see sparingly, golf is a way we bond to those we share our lives with.

Play more golf, make more friends, live a fuller life. Golf is a recipe for happiness.

" Golf is a gateway to meaningful companionship "

EFFORTLESS POWER

My grandfather is old school. His golf philosophies don't pair so well with those who subscribe to the game's modern approach.

Gramps believes more in "effortless power" than a "powerful effort." This way of swinging the club has suited him well in his life.

In over eight decades of playing the game, he's mastered his move through a constant dedication to golf. He still values accuracy over length and artistry to strength. Gramps sees the swing path as the key to shaping shots: something he still does well even at 87.

He has never been much for flash, because he knows the steady horse wins the race. Hitting fairways and greens are the key, and that's achieved by repetition. When Gramps plays, his strategies are consistent with his teachings. A smooth swing and good ball striking can yield low scores.

If it can still work for him, imagine what it can do for others who love to play. A round with Gramps is a study in the classical theories of golf. There's much to learn from his wisdom. I still benefit from every lesson.

NECESSARY EVIL

Summer is the season of aerification. Grounds crew punch small holes into beautiful putting surfaces as a means of beneficial destruction. The roots need room to breathe and grow! Despite the disappointment from every golfer who hears this procedure has happened at their favorite course, this process is a necessary evil.

The Swiss cheese greens may be unsavory in the short term, but these measures taken by the agronomy crew will yield a rewarding experience in the months ahead. The layers of sand deposited on the greens are also inconvenient to good putting, but the bumpy three-footer today will soon become a smooth-rolling paradise. With fast-growing grasses, the healing process is not so long.

" What we suffer through today will be celebrated in good time "

Though reviled by everyone who plays the game, aerification is the secret to happy customers later in the year. What we suffer through today will be celebrated in good time. We should salute the sand-filled holes and cheer the inconsistent rolls! They are only a temporary pain.

EARLY TEE TIMES

Is there anything more exciting than an early morning tee time? Rising anticipation makes it hard to sleep the night before. Springing from bed, it's tempting to go straight to the course in pajamas.

The glistening dew on the ground and pungent smell of fresh-cut grass are like sirens that lure the golfer into another adventurous round. The rising sun offers a warm and familiar environment that every addicted golfer longs to revisit. It's hard to resist the opportunity to fulfill that desire.

We habitually seek the dopamine rush that comes from striking the first tee shot of the day. The closer that feeling comes to dawn, the more intense its effect. We jump at the chance to play the game we love. What a treat to start a day in the bliss of such a wonderful game.

A LENGTHY ROLL

The long putt is viewed by many as something that should merely be survived. In this situation, most hope to two-putt and then move on to the next hole. Meanwhile, players of a different mindset see great opportunity when looking down the line of a lengthy roll.

Holing such a putt is the ultimate momentum builder. Not only can it change a round for the better, it may also flip a match. Watching a ball fall into the cup from great distance is sure to lift your spirit while also rattling your opponent.

It may sound silly to approach a putt of a few dozen feet in length with an aim to make it, but it's a clever strategy for the cunning golfer. The greens are the ultimate equalizer in this game. Everyone wants to pick up strokes with the flatstick, yet not enough players approach the effort with proper assertion. Any putt can be holed.

A good feel for the speed and line will build confidence. Trying to make such putts on the last roll is a smart play. In order to avoid a three-putt, it's better to aspire for precision. Aim small, miss small. Every golfer should strive to become an elite putter from across the green. It only takes a few long putts dropping to develop a sense of the importance of this skill. Once the long ones start going in, everything changes.

SIMPLE TRUTHS

Golf is a game populated by simple truths. I find great peace in that. When my world is filled with challenges and life puts me in a bind, I go to the golf course as a means of lifting my spirit. The uncomplicated nature of the game yields a deep sense of calmness in me.

There just isn't that much to figure out here. Throughout my whole existence, it has been the golf course where I am most myself. While shedding my worries and collecting my feelings, a walk down the fairway brings me back to center. The ups and downs of golf have little consequence beyond the confines of the course. Meanwhile, golf is the only place I can temporarily shelve the ups and downs of life. The difficulties of my day-to-day are not to be ignored, but the setting golf provides at least allows me to diffuse their more harmful nature.

In pursuit of a little ball, I am made free from the worst of my thoughts. The walk brings me clarity, too. Trying to post a good score leaves no room for other problems. I get to rest my mind here. Golf gives me an arena where everything just makes sense. For this, I am truly blessed.

❝ golf is the only place I can temporarily shelve the ups and downs of life ❞

BETWEEN GLORY AND DESPAIR

The difference between glory and despair is often marginal. The fate of a shot is decided in just a moment. With a breath being held and the ball falling slowly from the sky, it becomes apparent that the result is uncertain.

Watching closely, the golfer keenly focuses on every factor affecting the ball's flight: wind, humidity, and temperature—along with trajectory and velocity—all combine at once. These details occur in the tiny instant that a shot is underway. Hope isn't enough to overcome a slight miss, though. Even the smallest observation as a shot takes off can tell the ball-striker what their fate is.

We may add some body English as a desperate final push, but those needed inches won't quite come. The undesirable image of a shot that has fallen just short is a devastating blow. Like a misjudged rocket launch, the results seem catastrophic. The only solace from this outcome is knowing that the risk was worth taking. Those thrilling seconds are what make us feel alive, and that's why we play the game. Another opportunity will surely come again.

LOVE AND GOLF

A good friend once asked me for some advice on how to manage being a golf addict while also being a husband and father. There is no "one size fits all" solution, but I do believe in a few simple deeds that can help any diehard golfer stay married.

For starters, it's critical that you take time each and every day to tell your wife how much you love her. For me, I try to do this at least ten times a day, which isn't hard because it's my favorite thing to profess. Second, I believe it's important to share the game I adore with the people I love. My most special moments on the golf course are when I'm with my wife and daughter in the evenings: we make memories there that will forever fill me with joy. Finally, I have found that being gracious and thankful to my spouse for every chance I get to spend time on the golf course is imperative to keeping our relationship strong. Every minute I get to play golf is one she is an incredible partner to me.

I remember when we first began to date, and I confessed my golfing passions. She likely didn't know what she was in for, but because she loves me, she supports my passions, just as I try to do the same for her. Relationships are a two-way street, and in order to keep our individual selves alive, both parties have to give a lot. When golf is added to the equation, it can make that complicated at times.

I'm amazingly blessed to have a loving wife who inspires me to chase my dreams and supports those pursuits on a daily basis. The best advice I can give is to marry someone who you not only want to share a life with, but someone you can't imagine life without. If you have those things, the rest will work out pretty well.

A BOY IN SUMMER

When I was a young lad, summer meant long days on the golf course. From the first light of day until the moon appeared in the evening sky, I could be found with my friends playing our favorite game.

The walks were extensive, and matches seemed never ending. We only took breaks to have a swim in the pool or enjoy a candy bar and a coke on the clubhouse porch. Those days were magic, and I miss them dearly.

Now, as I'm older and bound by many commitments, my summer days are filled with different things. And yet, golf hasn't stopped pulling me into the sunshine. I find my time on the course after work or on weekends, still chasing my passion through the humidity and high temperatures of the season.

Of all the things I love about the game, my favorite may just be how it makes me feel like a kid. Whether I'm playing a few holes with my dog at dusk or walking with friends on a warm Saturday morning, I'm reminded of the joys I experienced in my adolescence.

The breaks I take now tend to include different beverages, and if I go to the pool, it's with my young family. That old magic hasn't left me, though. Golf fills my spirit and makes me smile, just like it did when I was a boy in summer.

"That old magic hasn't left me"

MY BIGGEST FAN

A father is many things for his children. He is a mentor, friend, caregiver, and supporter. Fathers are also fans. They root for their children to succeed both in life and in other ventures.

My dad has long been my biggest fan, and my brother's biggest fan as well. "Pops," as we call him, has been pulling for his boys in every endeavor since the days we became his sons. There is nobody else I know who yearns as much to see his kids prosper.

When we play golf, I've often thought that Pops cared more about watching us than playing himself. I've always thought that was pretty damn cool.

Pops can play a bit, too. He'll sneak up on us from time to time, but his biggest golf smiles happen when he gets to witness a tight match between his boys.

A hard-working guy, he has taught us many lessons on how to build a life, but his most important teachings have been on how to be a great father. If I had to boil his approach down to one simple idea, it would be this: always insist on the continued advancement of your children.

Pops has pushed us and coached us our whole lives. Both on and off the golf course, he still roots for his boys. It's great to know I have a fan like that.

THE FEEL PLAYER

Feel players seem to have a sixth sense for golf. Just prior to contact, there's a split second when they know whether everything is in order. To those who go on intuition, a swing is more than just an athletic motion: it's a sequence of events that are the result of a life's work.

Their 10,000 hours of practice have yielded an ability to know where the clubface is throughout the entire swing. When everything is in order, it's almost as if a smile starts to emerge just before impact. These players know what's about to happen before even taking a look.

it's a sequence of events that are the result of a life's work

With a grin, they watch the ball fly to the target, as all signs point to yet another successful shot. It's like a painter observing a finished portrait, a mechanic starting a defunct engine, a singer with perfect pitch hitting their note. It's the work of an artisan, driven by skill but achieved through feel. A display worthy of admiration.

WHY WE GO

A golf course is a place of refuge. A retreat, if you will. The places in which we play this game are far more than just grassy plains with obstacles scattered about. They are grounds fashioned for the enjoyment of life and contemplation of what our role might be in it.

The golf course is intended to be a friendly confine for sorting through the theories we've formed for the world. It's devised to help us remember why we are here. The holes we play allow us to discover who we are through the exploration of self. It's a good location to let go.

The golf course is somewhere we can be vulnerable, while still feeling safe. It's one of the few venues where we can be both released from our burdens and grounded in our reality. To feel those conflicts simultaneously is to know the boundaries of our existence.

We come with clubs in tow and play a game across these fields, which give us some room to wander. It's in the space between our swings that we are most mindful and appreciative of all that we've been given. To traverse these lands through our sporting habits is to be at peace.

We go to the course for so much more than golf.

THE LAST ONE ON THE COURSE

The last man on the course is easy to spot. Long after the parking lot clears and the pro shop is closed, he can be found still stalking the course.

His relationship with the game is unique to say the least. His preference for solitude leads to evenings sorting through the game and many other things.

He's not much for booking tee times: those don't matter at this hour. When he pulls up to play, the rest of the golfers he knows are sitting down for dinner.

The magic he finds in the final hour of his day is worth the sacrifice of other social interactions. Here he can search for his game in an uninterrupted environment. The only distractions he must mind are the rising sound of crickets and the fast-fading light.

A few extra chips and some practice putts are the hallmark of these quick trips around his favorite holes. An ever-present smile and a kind wave to anyone who drives by is further evidence that he is content. All he wants is to relish in such splendor. He can see most clearly just before dark.

A WORTHY PURSUIT

A round of golf is a series of thrilling moments strung together through a long walk. The most exciting are the ones found on courses that keep you guessing.

This game is intended to be an adventure. Thrills can come from bold tee shots and daring escapes. A well-struck approach, holed chip, or sidewinding putt can stir the blood as well. These are the sort of shots that make golf worth playing.

Because the game is hard, it's also compelling. The golfer's ability to overcome difficulties on the course is what makes the sport so addicting. Golf is a lifelong chase for fleeting thrills: a worthy pursuit for the sporting soul.

" Golf is a lifelong chase for fleeting thrills "

PLACEMAKING

Details matter. They are often the difference between good and great. In golf, the places that pay attention to the small things are more likely to provide a memorable experience.

From tee markers, to scorecards, to pin flags, and everything in between: the many elements of a golf course come together to create a sense of place. The aim should be to make a consistent theme and an attractive aesthetic.

This doesn't mean that courses should be cluttered: less is usually more. A discerning eye should determine whatever items are to be placed on or along the golf trail. For those pieces that make the cut, they should be seen as compelling elements of a story told through spaces.

The golfer should not be distracted by these details. Instead, they should allow us to further sink into a state of bliss and enjoyment. When properly executed, these details will create a stirring feeling that can compel us to return again in search of the same sensory activation.

Well-appointed detailing can make the seams of a golf course disappear. Small enhancements make a big difference; they both excite the familiar player and please the newcomer. The courses that fixate on these matters are often rewarded with the loyalty of their enthusiasts. A brief moment of interest leaves a lasting impression. These are the breadcrumbs that bring people back again and again.

THE GRANDEST VIEWS

God gives golfers all the best views. No other game or sport offers such wild and vivid vistas. The best hours for enjoying golf are those nearest the evening.

The possibility of colored skies at sundown is enough to bring any thrill-seeking player out for a look. We are blessed to have golf in our lives, for it helps us to appreciate the wonders of nature while enjoying a game made by man.

Golf is a means for exploring the creator's vision in many of the world's finest places. The well-balanced golfer pursues more than just thrilling moments from his or her play: they seek out the splendors of the earth.

There are many elements that make golf a spiritual game, and chief among them are the sunsets we are blessed to see.

A TRULY GREAT GOLF HOLE

A truly great golf hole is impossible to forget. From the first time you see it, something about your understanding of the game changes. It's not how you play it that's memorable, it's how the hole made you feel.

Sometimes, a single hole can become the spark for a larger interest in golf design. A study of course architecture can be a portal to a deeper appreciation for the game. For the uninitiated, it may seem like much ado about nothing, but it only takes one special place to change that outlook.

A great hole can serve as the key that unlocks this door. While trodding across certain fairways, a golfer's eyes can be opened to new ways of seeing the world. The elements of an intoxicating golf hole can speak volumes about the artistry involved in building such spaces.

The best holes have layers. Like a blistering chapter in a compelling novel, certain holes keep the interest up and the pages of the course turning. They stand out not only for their part of the routing, but also in the catalogue of golf memories in your mind.

This game offers an endless buffet of fascinating experiences. The more you seek to know about how and why holes are built certain ways, the more you'll find an appreciation for the places you play. It only takes falling in love with one hole to start that journey.

" it's how the hole made you feel "

A SMALLER GOLF EXPERIENCE

Golf doesn't have to be big. Even a small dose of this game can be enchanting. With the right ingredients, a few holes set on a modest scale can provide a lot of enjoyment.

People need places that inspire them to expand their presence in the game. There's also an increasing desire to play quickly. Such models require only minimal resources.

One of golf's most wonderful charms is the variety of its venues. With no set standards to define "what golf is," the sport can exist in so many different ways. Imagine the possibilities for bringing golf to the masses if more facilities existed that offer the game in an easily accessible way.

I can imagine small putting greens in urban settings, pitch-and-putts that weave through neighborhoods, and short courses on the edge of towns. There can be suburban driving ranges designed for short clubs only, or perhaps even a course of merely six holes that could be repeated accordingly. The possibilities seem rather endless.

Golf will thrive when the game is closer to where we live, more relatable to everyone who has an interest in it, and offered on a smaller and more approachable scale. As some are already proving: by shrinking the game, we might just grow it.

RITUALS AS EXPERIENCES

Rituals can create a memorable experience. In golf, there are many great examples of meaningful rituals.

A ritual can come in many forms. They often exist as a ceremony of sorts. These productions may be based on history or other stories that are unique to a place. Often found at resorts and elite clubs, golf-related rituals are a showcase of tradition. They can even represent the passage of time or a transition of leadership.

Competitions can be celebrated in this manner as well—either through a grand opening moment or with the elaborate presentation of trophies and awards. Rituals can include music, speeches, or other forms of performance.

Rituals should excite the senses and provide entertainment. They pair well with golf for many reasons, as golf's connections to nature and history have always made for good storytelling. A ritual sparks imagination and stirs the blood. When provided at regular intervals, they also create specific reasons for people to return to a place. For those who attend and observe them, rituals are a way to experience a shared memory, leaving us with yet another story to tell about our enjoyment of the game.

A COURSE TO CALL HOME

Most golfers spend their whole lives dreaming about courses they hope to see someday. Bucket lists are filled with the names of faraway links, exclusive clubs, and resorts in exotic locations. With so much time spent longing for other golf, it's easy for a player to forget the charms of the course they call home.

The shame of traveling for golf is that there's only so much time available to enjoy the spoils of a special course. Those limitations aren't present at home. Although the course down the street may not have as grand a setting or as illustrious a reputation, it does offer familiarity.

Getting to know a golf course on an intimate level is a privilege. It may be thrilling to know a new course on a surface level, but it's the place we play frequently that yields the greatest appreciation over time. It's good to dream and travel and play: this expands one's understanding of the game. But it's far more important to find a place where golf can be explored regularly. We need somewhere we can know by heart.

DREAMING OF THE COURSE

How many golfers go to bed dreaming of the first tee? It's hard to keep the eyes closed with golf on the brain.

There is no easier thing to wake up early for than a tee time at a beautiful golf course. In an increasingly tamed world, playing golf remains a thrilling adventure. For many, it's a splash of excitement that helps to break up the routines of everyday life.

In golf, we are allowed the chance to be the champion of our own destiny. For a few hours, every decision about what to do next falls squarely on us. To have that much control is a rare opportunity for most—another reason golf is so addicting.

What a glorious feeling to stand on the opening hole with club in hand, friends nearby, and infinite possibilities lying ahead. Golf offers the occasion to begin again. Fresh and unburdened, each round yields a sense of incredible freedom. It's no wonder we dream about this game so often.

Golf offers the occasion to begin again

THE NEXT AMERICAN PASTIME

Golf should be the next great American pastime. The game is widely available and can be enjoyed by anyone.

Golf is a means to connect us with our fellow citizens: no matter their age, sex, race, creed, or political persuasions. A shared love for golf brings people together.

Although a highly challenging game, the pleasures of golf are easily found anywhere it's played. Golf is a way to enjoy the outdoors, bond with friends, take a break, and test our own abilities. As a sport, golf offers an opportunity to compete against many opponents: the course, the elements, ourselves, and each other. Just as in life, golf shows that we are shaped by the obstacles we must navigate.

This is also a game for exploration. It can be played across nearly any landscape, and in many ways it's a showcase of our country's beauty. This is a most democratic game as well. Low score always wins. Anybody who is willing to put in the time can become a champion.

Good golf is something worth aspiring to, and as with our country, we have to work hard in order to reap its rewards. Golf teaches us perseverance, and there's no more American trait than that.

Above all else, golf is a way to be free. It grants those who play it the chance to roam and enjoy some time for the betterment of self. For millions of Americans, golf is a miniature pursuit of happiness. What better way could we Americans relax than with a game that so often mirrors our national ethos?

THE OPENING MOVE

A tee shot is like an opening move on the chessboard. Each hole is a new game, and there are many ways to win. The opponent is always par.

A well-placed drive sets up the board for other successful moves. Attempted shortcuts can result in a quick defeat. In order to conquer par, you have to execute a series of moves. The best strategy is to start with one that plays to your strengths while leaving many options on the table.

A good tee shot is one that allows for the next swing to be decisive. A stumble on the first swing isn't a death sentence, but it makes capturing the board more difficult. An unassuming, yet appropriately executed drive can lead to a wide array of options. Proper positioning makes a swift attack possible.

When the winning move comes, we can trace it back to the preceding drive. Beating par begins with the first move.

THE $1 BUNKER LESSON

I remember when my grandfather taught me how to escape from a bunker. He instructed me to put a dollar bill beneath the ball, with the orb resting on George Washington's head. "Blast the bill out from under the ball," he told me. That's it. That was the lesson.

Bunkers strike fear in so many, yet as Gramps taught me, there's no reason for that. The proper shot from the sand is much simpler than it seems. An open clubface, wide stance, and a turn through the shot is all that's required. Using the dollar bill is a surefire way to learn good form.

To this day, when I find myself in a bunker, I still imagine a note of legal tender beneath my ball. I can recall hitting such shots as a kid. With an explosion of sand, the ball would fly out toward the target, and as the dust settled, a dollar would slowly flutter back to the ground.

Through many repetitions of this drill, I learned to approach bunkers with a sense of confidence. Hit the dollar hard and let the club do the work. This simple instruction can make anyone a better bunker player. It'll only cost you a buck.

LOST IN THE WOODS

The woods aren't well-suited for golf. It's best to avoid playing from there. Unfortunately, we all find our way into the trees from time to time. That's when we must call on our scrambler's instinct.

Knowing how much of the tree line to take on is a gut feeling. It helps to have been there before. Trial and error is the only way to master the punchout strategy.

Confidence plays an important role here. To successfully emerge from the timber stand, it's wise to select a route that minimizes the damage. A smart golfer plays the odds. Sometimes the risky path is tempting, but the most important objective is to get out of the woods. The goal is to find a way to advance to the next best scenario.

Good scores perish when wannabe heroes try to craft an overzealous escape plan. The winning mindset is to save the bold shot for when the peril is past. If lost in the woods, find the quickest way out to the fairway, and play hard from there. Get out while you still can!

The goal is to find a way to advance to the next best scenario

A VISUAL EXPLORATION

I enjoy golf courses that afford me the opportunity to see beyond just the hole I'm on. An ideal routing should include various vistas that showcase the best aspects of the land. I love to look over ridges, back down corridors, across other fairways, and through the canopies of trees. Golfers should be invited through design to observe the many characteristics of a place.

It's incredibly enjoyable to finish a golf walk and feel as if I saw the property in full. When given the chance to play a course many times, I like to identify the best places on the course to capture its natural essence—often those occur while standing on one hole and looking at another.

Golf is a game for reflection, and while we are contemplating the depths of this sport, we should also consider the wonders in front of us. I want to see how a hole fits into the larger picture. To best understand the puzzle, it's good to see it from many angles. I adore the well-designed courses that give me these stunning visual moments needed to do so.

The most unexpected revelations happen when we look away from the target. I do not want to simply be on a golf hole, I long to be a visual explorer.

A LIFE WITHOUT GOLF

I've often sat and wondered what my life would be like without golf. Upon reflection, it's clear that I would have a vastly different existence.

I wouldn't have the same friends, and I'd likely live somewhere far from home. The nearness I have forged with my family may have become distance instead. I would lack the skills to build close relationships, and I'd likely fall back into my former introverted self.

There are so many places I would've never visited, and countless experiences I would've missed. Peace of mind would easily escape me, and the man I used to be may still be going about his old ways. Surely, I wouldn't speak to God as much.

There would be no outlet for my passions, and I would have missed a thousand beautiful walks. I also doubt my dog would like me as much. There would be no place to let my soul roam free, and I shudder to imagine how lost my dreams would be. My life would lack a proper escape from stress, as regular meditation would just sound silly to me.

Without golf, there would be far fewer good memories, and my life would be lessened by the absence of everyday laughter. My sense of accomplishment would be dashed, and my sporting hopes would have gone unfulfilled, too.

There would be no understanding of the joy that comes from a good swing, a fortunate bounce, or a holed putt. I would have learned much less about how to carry on in this world, and I never could quite know myself in full.

There wouldn't be much to write about either.

It's hard to imagine my life without golf, because golf has been my life. If the game was not there to shape me, I would be defined by something entirely different.

Fortunately, I have golf, and it most certainly has me. I've undoubtedly been made better by golf, and I like to believe the game has been made better by me.

Golf is simply who I am.

HIT IT AND HOPE

During the height of summer, when the rough grows thick, it's easy to find your ball in a flyer lie.

When you hit a shot from such a place, the ball behaves in strange ways. Spin seemingly disappears, turning into a knuckleball effect. A well-hit shot can appear to defy gravity and just sail through the sky with nothing to slow it down.

Lacking direction, the ball will look like it's floating as it sails well past the intended target. This makes judging these lies incredibly difficult. Having little control over how the ball reacts to your swing is both a challenge and a frustration.

Sometimes all you can do is hit it and hope for the best.

HELP THEM HAVE FUN

Children, like everyone else, are drawn to things they enjoy. The easiest way to teach golf to kids is to help them have fun with the game.

Take them with you, but don't take things so seriously. Laugh, and smile, and help them find a spark of curiosity.

Talk about why golf is fun to play. When a kid can learn the game in an environment that brings them joy, they are much more likely to stay with it. There's a reason we call it "playing" golf. Let them see that side of the game!

Show a child how golf is meant for having fun, and you could unlock a lifetime of passion for the sport. Once they discover how golf can make them happy, the rest should take care of itself.

"you could unlock a lifetime of passion for the sport"

THE BEST SORT OF GOLFER

There is much to admire about a golfer. No two are alike, yet they likely share many positive characteristics. The best of this sort provides a good model for others to follow.

Golfers are persistent and aren't easily deterred. They are confident and committed. A golfer is a fighter, always pressing even when the odds are stacked against them. They are focused and filled with drive. Golfers make for good friends and great storytellers. They seek adventure in their lives and are always eager to learn. Golfers are at home in nature and have a great appreciation for the land used for their game. They are competitors and sporting enthusiasts. The golfer is probably well-mannered and congenial, too. The game demands much from those who play it, and a proper golfer strives to live up to those high standards.

The golfer that exhibits these qualities should be celebrated. They are worthy of emulation by us all.

THE QUIET OF TWILIGHT

Quiet is vastly underrated. As wonderful as it is to be surrounded by friends and loved ones in a jovial golf environment, it's equally pleasing and perhaps more rewarding to be alone and silent in nature.

To hear nothing but the sounds of the evening on a golf course is a considerable treat. Sensory overload has become such a common reality in our world that it's easy to forget what quiet truly sounds like. A golf course is still a good place to find that.

Beneath the last light of day, when the birds have settled down and the crickets have yet to come out, there's a window of time when all noise seems to cease. No voices, phones, cars, or other stressful reminders. It's amazing how much can fade away during a few minutes like that.

Regardless of the distractions in their day, wise golfers have sought to enjoy such moments for centuries. Yet, because of its increasing rareness, the quiet offered by golf has never been worth more. It makes me wonder why the twilight rate is such a steal. I'd pay any price to find more of that bliss.

it's easy to forget what quiet truly sounds like

A GAME FOR BUILDING COMMUNITY

All my favorite places for golf have one great thing in common. They are more than just courses: they are communities.

This game has the ability to nurture relationships in ways that are uncommon to other pastimes. Golfers become attached to a community when they feel a deep connection with both the place and the people who spend time there. There are thousands of golf courses across the world, but most don't achieve this distinction.

A true golf community is found where there's a palpable love for the game. You know them when you see them. It's easy to notice when friendship is an ever-present virtue, and the good days are measured in smiles, not scores. In such a place, people not only come to play, they gather for the purpose of finding valuable companionship.

Serving as a beacon for kindred spirits, these courses stir the golfer's soul. Every day spent in this kind of company is a dream come true. This is the sort of golf that inspires evangelists for our game. We should seek these places out and aim to replicate their magic.

OUR FEET SHOW US THE WAY

When we walk a golf course, we find things that otherwise prove elusive. We find quiet, calmness, and a deeper connection to nature. There are also many personal revelations found along the trail.

Our best thoughts are made more apparent through the steps we take. As we walk around a golf course, we also walk around the thoughts and feelings that populate our mind. Golf is a search for answers, and very few of them have much to do with the game being played.

Golf is a search for answers

The walking golfer is looking for something else entirely. We go on walks as a means to sort through our troubles and come up with a scheme for what may come next in life. With each pace we make, clarity becomes more attainable. Through golf, we seek to find the next iteration of ourselves one step at a time. Our feet show us the way forward.

DAMN, THAT'S PRETTY

Every now and then, I'll come across a small corner of a golf course that gives me pause. I'll think to myself: "Damn, that's pretty."

A well-designed golf hole can feel like a painting brought to life. What other game gives us the chance to observe such a full canvas of nature?

I enjoy it when a course offers me recurring vignettes of splendid scenery. It's a blissful experience to see these expressions of the land's character as I explore the property. What greater pleasure can golf offer us than to be a guide for the wonders of our world?

There are many ways to judge a golf course, but the easiest measure might be whether it's pleasing to the eye. An attractive setting will always appeal. Even an average course in a pretty place will usually fare well. Nice views and a pleasant walk will lure me in every time.

A SUNDAY STROLL

I've spent many Sundays strolling across golf courses. There's something about the last day of the week that makes my outings more relaxed. Perhaps knowing there are people praying in the morning, or families gathering for food and fun in the afternoon, that makes me think of joy and happiness. Things just seem more right on Sunday.

Golf has long played an important role in my life, and the walks I've taken on Sundays have yielded many cherished memories. Growing up, after the last hymnal was finished and lunch had been served, golf was always the next thing on the agenda. I still find elements of that in my life.

Golf is a soulful game. It gives us the chance to find serenity in a world where that can often seem out of reach. On Sundays, my pace is slower and my posture is at ease. My swing seems more graceful, too. Worries dissipate, and putts roll truer. There's a pleasantness that permeates through the course, and golfers tend to be extra appreciative of both the game and all they have been given. Surely God's grace plays a part in that.

People playing golf on a Sunday genuinely appear to be in a peaceful state. It certainly has that effect on me. Sunday makes everything better. It's my favorite day for golf.

THE WALK IS MORE REWARDING

Summer is when the walking golfers show their true colors. It's easy to opt in for a stroll when it's a breezy 75 degrees outside, but when the heat index clears triple digits, the diehards tend to stand out.

It takes a certain commitment to carry your clubs under the blazing summer sun. Despite the convenience of taking a cart, it's better to test your stamina and take a hike instead. The sweat is good for you, and there's a rush that comes from tarrying across the course in blistering conditions.

Walking is addictive, and it yields a sense of accomplishment. In summer, the steps mean ever more. It only takes a few rounds in a cart to lose your pace and fall into the trap of riding. Stay true to your convictions and take the course in stride. Walking will always be worth the work. Even beneath a relentless sun, the game remains best enjoyed by foot.

> " Walking will always be worth the work "

GOLFERS ARE INSANE

Let's admit it: we golfers can be a little insane. We will brave nearly any scenario and face unimaginable consequences just for the chance to hit a great shot. No matter what forces may reign upon us, we insist on playing through.

For centuries our kind has fought battles with nature and wars against our better judgment, all for the opportunity to chase a little ball. It defies logic. There are no ways to adequately describe such madness.

The golfer's soul is tormented by a deep-rooted desire to play the game, no matter what else is happening. Dodging lightning, missing family dinners, and denying the demands of one's conscience are all par for the course. Good decisions don't seem to live around these parts.

Golfers understand the brevity of life, and they don't care much for advice that demonizes risk. It's not so much that the game is well-suited for squirrelly personas, but instead, people of a certain character are attracted to golf for its risks and rewards. No common sense or force of nature can seem to keep the golfer at bay. We play on. Not even the rains of Noah could wash out the need to make a few good swings.

The golfer never stops.

WE ARE THE SWINGS WE MAKE

We are a personification of the swings we make. In a lifetime spent pursuing the joys of golf, we slowly become an embodiment of the game itself.

Golf is a lifestyle, and given time, it will consume us. From the clothes we wear, to the friends we have and the trips we take, golf shapes everything we do.

Golf takes our money and our time, and eventually everything else. But it also keeps us from being sedentary.

This most addictive game always gives us something to be interested in. Boredom is a foreign concept to those who always keep their clubs nearby.

Golfers are passionate people, and it's best to direct that energy into something that gives us purpose.

Golf is a driving force for change in many a troubled heart. Because of the longevity we enjoy in this pastime, golf can be an endless source for self-improvement.

As a sporty endeavor, golf gives those of us who play it an uncapturable target in life. Having a constant objective is a good way to keep the mind sharp and the soul in good spirits.

We never stop tinkering with our game or working to better ourselves. Those who overlook golf's true meaning miss this point entirely. Days spent on the course and hours pounding away on the range aren't done in vain. Our real practice is spent learning about ourselves. We are the swings we make.

STANDING TALL IN THE SHORT GRASS

The first few hundred yards of a golf walk are always an interesting hike. Depending on the opening tee ball, those steps can either be easy and confident, or frantic and shaky. How we start doesn't always determine how we finish, but it damn sure sets the tone.

❝ How we start doesn't always determine how we finish, but it damn sure sets the tone ❞

The path up the fairway is highly desirable, while the hazard-laden routes are riddled with demons. A good start can yield early confidence, especially while opponents are wandering through the woods. Don't let your guard down, though: the next shot still requires a good swing. There's no better place to take it from, either. It feels good to walk tall on the short grass.

SHARE THE GAME

Golf is a game for families. People who think otherwise are either blind to the real beauties of the game or part of the reason it gets a bad rap.

I spend a great deal of time on the golf course with my family, and those hours bring me endless smiles. I know of and have connected with many others who feel the same way.

The simple elements of golf—being in nature, laughing at failure, finding unexpected success, and enjoying nearness to others—are all qualities that are worthy of sharing with family. There are times reserved for matches and medal play, and even fun with friends, but there's no time more suited to showcasing the best attributes of golf like that spent with loved ones.

Golf is meant to be shared with those we are closest to. If we share a life with our family, we should also share this most special game with them. It's a wonderful thing to witness the happiness of my child and the excitement of my wife when we come together as a family on a golf course. There are few experiences I love more. This is the version of golf that I'm increasingly drawn to. It's the game I want to play for my lifetime. A golf family is a fine thing to be.

WATCHING IT FLY

When the ball sails through the sky, and your eyes focus on the fast-flying sphere, there's a feeling of calm that comes from confirming its direction.

There's both pride and peacefulness found in delivering the ball to its target. But it's more than just appreciating the result of a particular swing. The seasoned player quietly celebrates the success of each shot, because they remember all the work and time it took to realize it.

Achievements in golf aren't measured in swings, holes, and scores: it's in the years spent crafting your game that count most. Golf is for the patient. Dedication matters. The difference between good and great comes from devotion.

Golf is a practice. You can never perfect it, but you can learn to play the game with great proficiency. It's not easy, but the work is worth it. The payoff happens each time you find a fairway, hit the green, and hole a putt. That's why you stare down each and every result. You earned that view.

"The difference between good and great comes from devotion"

ANTICIPATE THE AMAZING

Golfing glory is found through all sorts of shots. If you play the game long enough, its magic will find you in many different ways.

More than a few times in every golfing life, there will be moments that defy logic. The ball will find its way to the hole and send shockwaves through your nervous system. There's no way to anticipate the amazing.

In an instant, what began as just another round can become a memorable outing you'll never forget. When the unexpected happens, the celebration rings out, and cheers rise among friends. Arms are raised for the accomplishment of rare feats, and all the bad shots you've ever hit seem worth it. The smiles will last for some time, but the overwhelming joy of such a shot is fleeting.

There's still more golf to play and many swings to make. After the thrill of a tremendous shot subsides, the hunt for the next bit of glory begins. You'll find it again, but only when you least expect it.

LET THE HILL BE YOUR FRIEND

Downhill lies require an elevated level of attention. It's the alignment that's the hardest thing to get right. Being on a slope makes for interesting golf, but without proper consideration, a misfired shot can easily become the result.

It's in these unbalanced situations where good feel pays off. Developing an ability to position the body in line with the camber of the ground is key. You can't fight the hill; you have to swing with it.

Through your feet, torso, and shoulder, there must be a sense of connection to the angle where the ball lies. By creating one continuous plane, you can swing in a normal fashion and generate an impressive result.

Those who overthink this scenario are bound to make a mistake. By calibrating your body to respond to the incline, a good turn is all that's needed. The trajectory may be influenced, of course, but the only thing that matters is where the ball winds up. Despite what may look like a daunting ball position, the results can work in your favor if you just get lined up properly. Let the hill be your friend.

IF YOU CAN SEE IT, YOU CAN DO IT

In golf, we can shape our outcomes, but first we must believe. In order to produce a desired result, we have to be able to clearly see what we want.

Our abilities are only limited by the strength of our imagination. To execute a shot, we have to envision what it should be. Its shape, distance, and trajectory must all be mapped out in the mind before we even select a club. The swing is merely a means for bringing our vision to life.

Once we have seen the shot play out in our thoughts, we simply have to allow it into existence. Affirmations of this sort are powerful tools for the golfer. With a profound belief in our ability and a clear picture of what we want to produce, any shot can be achieved. When we see it, we can do it.

IF YOU CAN SEE IT

NO END IN SIGHT

Every time I walk a golf course, I learn more about my presence in the world. Through my decades in this game, I've come to have a thorough understanding of what my best and worst qualities are. They often emerge from me as different personas.

My daily life can seem like a seesaw, with those angels and demons sitting on each side. Golf is how I measure which one is more dominant. But when I play, a sort of rebalancing happens.

By looking inside, I can find the levers I need to adjust in order to bring me closer to my better self. This is important work. In order to do it I need quiet, calm, and peaceful surroundings. Focus matters, too. A golf course is ideal for such reflection.

The walk leads me back to my more admirable self. I'm still learning how to improve, so I keep coming back to golf. It's a journey with no end in sight.

" Every time I walk a golf course, I learn more about my presence in the world "

AFTER THE EVENING RAIN

After the evening showers pass, some golfers look for a bit of practice before dark. The all-clear signal is made by clouds that turn the most peculiar shade of orange. There in the atmospheric cocktail shaker, light blends with the leftover moisture, releasing a unique spectrum of color before nightfall. In these final minutes of a once-rainy day, there's somehow still time for a few swings beneath this fiendish sky. Only the committed know these colors, though, acquainted through years of dedication.

It's good to hit some while you can. Every rep counts, and the colors are certainly worth seeing.

A GOOD GOLF PARTNER

Finding good golf friends is an important part of the game. In some ways, it's a lot like dating: you'll play with lots of people before you find the right fit.

It's good to look for players with similar interests and skill sets, but it may be even more valuable to discover an elevated sense of humor. A need for adventure and fellowship is rather important, too.

Some partners will come and go, but over time there will be a few that you just can't shake. Through many walks, the experiences you share become strong bonds. The memorable swings and competitive matches keep things interesting, while the bad shots and head-shaking jokes ensure no round is a bore.

Golf friends make for cheap entertainment, but they can be costly to keep. They'll make you take trips, lose bets, and overextend bar tabs. It's all worth it, though. To have a group of golfers that seek to enjoy the world together is a wonderful thing. The laughs, chats, and long evenings celebrating the game are exactly why golf is so essential.

The time spent searching for friendship is always worth it. We need partners in golf just as we do in life.

CLOSE TO THE CUP

The best place to teach a new golfer how to play the game is right by the hole. They need to learn the most essential skill first. Give them a putter and help them figure out how to get the ball in the cup.

Start small. There's not much point in taking full swings until they develop some putting ability. This may sound counterintuitive, but it isn't. Beginners may see putting as the odd part of golf, and less thrilling than making contact with a driver, but it's actually the more foundational portion of the game. Learning to make short putts is bound to produce more smiles than frowns.

Getting the ball in the hole is the object of golf, and that's ultimately achieved with the flat stick. When someone learns this first, it changes how they see the larger game. So many players never figure out how to finish a hole, and that makes the game less enjoyable. Teach someone how to become a putter, and they'll grow into a golfer. Start with what matters most.

THE GRIND NEVER ENDS

Most golf rounds are a grind. Every shot is a battle against bogey, and it's hard to stay in that mindset hole after hole. For the majority of amateurs, though, managing misses is just a way of life.

Finding a way to turn off-center swings into a string of pars is a real skill. Honestly, it's much more impressive than a monotonous player hitting fairways and greens. It takes constant concentration to keep scores low when the ball doesn't behave the way you'd like.

Through some combination of strategy and scrambling, pars can be manufactured from a myriad of challenging positions. Leaving shots in places with room to recover is key. Steering away from hazards and staying below the hole are smart moves, too. We are often in a state of recovery.

Golfers who make many birdies set themselves up with booming drives and accurate approaches. The par-saver makes their hay by knowing where misshits are most likely to go.

Chips, putts, punches, and sand saves are all important parts of that repertoire. The best grinders take a great deal of pride in this work. And it most certainly is work.

There are indeed days when things go more according to plan, but the law of averages usually yields an outing with many challenges. In this reality, golf can often feel more like a mining operation than leisure. There's much to appreciate about hard-fought pars.

It's good to be a grinder.

Dogs see us for what we really are. Short tempered, rowdy, and confused. I think they also see how golf helps us overcome those things. They know we aren't right, but they stay by our side nonetheless.

There is no way they can understand the complex concepts of golf. But somehow there's an understanding of why we play it. They can comprehend our need for space and play.

Even across the communication divide that exists between species, dogs can sense that we too have a desire to roam. We're not so different in that respect. The calmness dogs provide golfers is greatly under appreciated. Dogs will forgive our behavior and have empathy for our missteps. We can all benefit from that sort of companionship.

GIVE IT ALL YOU'VE GOT

Some golf holes require a mighty swing. On these holes, in order to score well, a bold move must be made. Every course should have a moment or two that challenges the limits of a player's ability.

A smooth turn works in most instances, but certain holes demand a bit more gusto. A big carry or sharp dogleg may be the instigating scenario here.

There is always a high risk of failure in these tense situations. Hazards and hills and water and waste areas may be scattered about, and for many who pass, doom may seem certain. But knowing that an ejection can occur is a powerful motivation to abandon any trepidation and focus.

There's only one way to manage the heroic shot. With no safe harbor in sight, you must conjure a confident swing to overcome an uncertain result. You need to make a decisive strike to avoid the potential pitfalls placed on the hole.

These shots will cause all sorts of trouble for those who can't stay focused. Too much thinking will turn things sideways in a hurry. It's better to grab a trusted club and swing it with authority. Make a lashing blow down and through the ball. Move onward to the target with a high finish and hope for a fine result.

Shots like these are what make golf interesting. Give it everything you got.

START YOUR DAY WITH GOLF

Golf in the morning is sure to make any day much improved, especially if it happens before work.

There's something about dew-sweeping rounds that make me want to get things done. Maybe it's the sights and sounds of the course coming together around me. Meditations under a morning sun are good for focusing the mind. It only takes a few holes to get my conscience in line with my ambitions, and from that clarity emerges a strategy for the day

Golf is an underrated method for charting a productive day. As much as I adore ending my evenings on the course, starting a day there is a different sort of dopamine hit. Instead of relaxing after work, the object of the early morning outing is more akin to a check-up on my determination.

With a full schedule ahead, I play at a quickened pace. Finishing on time is the first accomplishment of the day. Getting my heartrate up helps to set the tone for work later. In this sense, dawn patrol is a wonderful window of time for golf. When there's much to do, those hours may be the only ones available for the game.

I've often profited from such walks, when all I could do is swing, walk, and repeat in a timely way. In those dew-covered steps, I find a rhythm for my daily requirements. Work starts as soon as I start thinking about it, and a few holes with coffee is a great way to set the cadence of a busy day.

The focus I need for golf is easily transferred to other projects. If I can scratch my itch for this early, then the rest of the day is left to get things done.

A SINGULAR THOUGHT

A golf swing only lasts a second, but in that moment many thoughts can pass.

Too much thinking gets in the way of good golf. A quiet mind is best, yet it may be helpful to concentrate on a single idea to keep others at bay. Finding one element of the swing to keep in mind creates a focus for your thoughts. The simpler the concept, the better.

For example, I like to focus on my breathing. If I can remember to exhale on my takeaway each time, then there isn't much room in that moment for other destructive thoughts. If I can fill my mind with a singular concept, then I might be able to pull off the swing without interference. By the time I take my breath, the ball is on its way.

All you need is one little notion. Save the complex thinking for the walks instead.

MEMBER-GUEST SEASON

I'm not sure who first invented the idea of member-guest golf tournaments, but I'm sure glad they did. Some of my favorite golf memories have been born from the long, laugh-filled days of these competitions. It's hard to have a bad time while engrossed in such an indulgent environment.

When invited to play, I jump at the chance to participate. It's a lot of fun to get lost in golf for a weekend and make new friends. These club tournaments are marked by heavy pours, interesting personalities, and tense putts. The food spread is obscene, and the smack talk is turned up to the highest level. No matter the format, it's always a good way to compete with kindred spirits.

You've got to really love golf to spend that much time and money on it in a 48-hour window. The member/guest experience was made for the golf junkie, and I'm unquestionably part of that crowd. I've been on some winning teams but most of my member-guest record is defined by side splitting jokes, bets that don't pay out, and playing as much as I can before having to return to the daily routine.

Being in the mix is always exhilarating, but the real enjoyment comes from the people I meet and the places I get to know better. No two events are the same, and I wish I could get to play them all. Member-guest tournaments always leave me with a small headache and a smile: signs of a good time had by all. It's a scene that suits me well.

GOLF FOR THE PEOPLE

Municipal courses are the backbone of American golf. These are places built for the people. For over a century, publicly owned and operated courses have been the breeding ground for passionate players and lifelong lovers of the game.

Munis make up a significant amount of our nation's golf landscape and they come in all shapes and sizes. Some are short and scruffy and filled with quirk, while others are big and brawny and immaculately manicured. They have one unifying commonality: anyone can play them. What a beautiful ideal to uphold!

Municipal golf has seen both good times and bad in America. In most places they teeter in between. Some would have them shuttered, claiming that the land and money should be put to better use. However, there are also millions of people who are willing to fight for their ability to enjoy public golf.

The game means too much to too many for municipal facilities to become defunded. That doesn't mean it will be easy to keep them open and improve their experiences, but this is America … it's not supposed to be easy. Municipal golf only works when we demand that it does. Like most elements of our

golf is for everyone

democracy, we must insist that our leaders listen, learn, and act, if we are to preserve the benefits of public golf.

Municipal courses matter in so many ways, and it's up to those who use, need, and support them to help share that truth. That starts with putting some skin in the game and getting involved. Ask yourself, what can I do for my muni?

Above all else, golfers need to promote the benefits and beliefs that drive public golf. Municipal courses uphold an important promise that's fundamental to the future of the game: golf is for everyone. It's a creed that should be proudly shared across our country. Those of us who want these courses to thrive should proclaim our support and show our dedication to this cause.

GREATNESS IS RELATIVE

The mid-handicap golfer has the hardest time making a leap to the next level. While higher-handicapped players can experience fast improvement through practice and instruction, a single-digit index can often feel more like a plateau.

It takes a significant amount of time and thought to get down to scratch. Most decent players don't have the time to develop the skills. The best way for someone to find those desired gains is through smarter course management.

With careful consideration, a mid-handicapper can shoot lower scores by eliminating mistakes. Where our skills may be limited, proper strategy can make up the difference. Finding a stock shot and using it to maneuver around the course is key. Positioning for par should always be top priority.

When finding both fairway and green becomes more regular, so will lower scores. Taking big numbers out of play is a big deal, too. Keeping the course in front of you and scoring through avoidance is a great way to maximize your game. It takes a tactician's mindset.

A mid-handicap player can shoot near or better than par if they are simply willing to become a best-in-class strategist. Golf is a thinking game, and when a good player learns to sharpen their mindful tools, they can have a real breakthrough. Greatness is relative, and there's more than one way to find it.

SOME CONCENTRATION
REQUIRED

Hitting tee shots offline is a surefire way to build focus as a golfer. That's because the recovery shot has to have your full attention.

Having spent years in the trees and beyond, I've learned how to hit all sorts of fancy shots. Necessity breeds innovation, I suppose. Because my chances at par have been so often dependent on this sort of swing, I've discovered how to center my attention on the shot at hand. In order to carve the ball around trees, punch through small openings, and hit fast-moving stingers, I can't let my mind slip.

Over time, that focus has carried over into the rest of my game. Survival skills are an important part of evolution, and the same holds true for golf. When I have to pull a great shot out of thin air, my focus tends to get pretty sharp. It's amazing what you can accomplish when you feel like you don't have any other option.

Every miss is just an opportunity to get the next one right. If you can take the concentration on a recovery shot back out into the fairways, good things will start to happen.

It's amazing what you can accomplish when you feel like you don't have any other option

THE BEST VICE IMAGINABLE

There's a lot to love about golf. Of all the vices available to get hooked on, it must be one of the best.

The fact that this game can be played at virtually any age makes it particularly compelling. Every time I tee it up with my grandfather, I'm reminded of this.

Even at his ripe old age, he still exudes a passion for the game. It's so clearly a major part of who he is that it's impossible to separate the man from the golfer. His love for golf is ever present, and that's a good thing to be known for. Building a life in golf is a great aspiration, and Gramps has shown me the blueprint for how to do it.

Because golf can be enjoyed at every stage of life, our relationship with it evolves as we age. That's why golf can be whatever we need it to be. When Gramps was young golf was a competition, when he was building a family it became a job, after retirement it was a way to be with grandkids, and now as he enjoys his days of leisure, golf is a pastime.

Golf is a game that never stops giving. There's nothing else quite like it, and someday I hope I can look back upon my golf experiences and appreciate just how much I got from them. I see that in Gramps, and he inspires me to do the same.

WORK/LIFE/GOLF BALANCE

There's a lot of talk about work/life balance, but for some, a work/life/golf balance is important, too. With that in mind, my friends and I get together on Tuesday evenings each week for nine holes of fast-paced competition.

When the clock hits 5pm, everyone shuffles their papers, closes their laptops, and turns off the office lights before making a mad dash to the course. With a few bucks in our wallets and hope for birdies in our heart, we set out to conquer our home course before dinner.

Our families are kind enough to grant us this weekly reprieve from the evening chores, and for a few hours the emails can wait. We enjoy cold beers and one another's fellowship. Tuesday night golf makes for a fine mid-week escape. It's the perfect respite from conference calls and daycare pickup.

A couple of hours with our pals helps to power through the week, and it's a great incentive to get things done at home or the office. Over the course of our brief round, there are hoots, hollers, fist pumps, and friendly banter. Sometimes the golf is good, and on other occasions we just shrug our shoulders and keep swinging. The game is on no matter the weather, and we are always on a mission to get home before dark.

Once we finish, the realities of our world return, and thoughts of the rest of the week comes rushing back. The golf makes for a fun break, though. We may not win any cash, but we always walk away with a big smile.

That's the sort of balance every golfer seeks. A little bit of golf makes every week better.

THE ENDLESS SEARCH

Every time we swing a club, there are endless possibilities for what can happen. Some shots turn out swell, while others fall short of expectations. As frustrating as the misses may be, it's that variety that keeps the golfer coming back.

In every golfer, there's an unquenchable desire to do better. That's why we all keep swinging. The only way to find glory in this game is to put in the reps. The more we play, the more rewards we can yield.

Of course, as the years and rounds go by, all those good and bad shots tend to blur together. What remains are memories of time well spent in pursuit of a passion. Our greatest swings turn out to be just an excuse to keep looking for more. What we really seek is the pleasure of an endless search. All those iterations eventually become a lifetime of joy.

NIGHT PUTTING

In my life, I've spent a lot of late nights on the putting green. Growing up in a small town meant that my friends and I often had to entertain ourselves. In a place with little to do, putting contests were our regularly scheduled programming.

We'd roll for dollars while the sun sank down, and we'd stay to settle up under the parking lot lights. Sometimes we brought the dogs, and on occasion our parents even got in on the game. Now that we've grown up, we still go to the green to pass the time.

The bets have gone up in value and the Coca-Cola has turned into beer, but the camaraderie is still of the same flavor. Over some tense three footers, we talk life and golf. Not much has changed in that sense.

The dogs may be different now, but the reason for being there is the same. Passing some time on the putting green with friends never gets old. It's still the best entertainment a few dollars can buy.

WHAT'S BETTER THAN THIS?

"What could we be doing that's better than this?" It's a good question to ask.

When we find ourselves enjoying golf in the late afternoon with friends and family, it's hard not to wonder why we don't do it more.

The peacefulness found in these outings make it easy to remember the true beauty of golf. We become relaxed in the most wonderful of ways, and through our wide-open eyes, the world seems to glisten.

It's always special to be in nature and with those whose presence we treasure. It warms the soul and calms the heart. How tragic that we don't insist on this relief more often.

In those moments, the world moves at a trickling pace, and for a few hours we can see just how good life can be. To play golf is to pause conflict. The combination of grassy fields, soaring clouds, and the flora and fauna before us seem to erode all worldly tension. We fill that void with smiles, laughter, small talk, and other visible signs of joy. As we play, we can't help but ponder why we aren't together like this every day.

Our time on earth is minuscule, and if the best of it happens on a golf course, why wouldn't we make a habit of it? The only real barrier is how we chose to spend what little time we have.

TOURNAMENT GOLF

Tournament golf is different. There's an elevated tension in the air and a sense of meaning in every shot.

It takes focus, deep breathing, and calm nerves to compete. Building a round through small wins is a smart strategy. Fairways and greens are the target. Hit them frequently, and the score will mostly take care of itself. In that mindset, the only thing that matters is the shot at hand.

Staying in each moment is key. You can't give any thought to the swings that have passed. It's a grind, and the only way to be successful is to remain concentrated on each unique situation.

Optimism and confidence come from keeping your head up, and your eyes forward, looking for the opportunities. Each good shot unlocks the next.

The way to win is to play against the course. The tournament conditions may be tough, but with the proper thought process, great things can happen.

GOLF SAVED MY LIFE

I've been known to tell folks that "golf saved my life." It's true.

Coming back to this wonderful game reminded me of childhood joy and helped me make my peace with God. Because of golf, I became less of a lost soul. Perhaps it was some combination of quiet walks with my dog and the camaraderie of friends found through the game that led me to discovering my better self.

I believe that people need both passion and purpose in their life, and through the years, golf has offered me both. Every time I'm on a golf course, I come a little closer to the person I hope to be.

Golf is an aspirational game, especially in the sense that it provides a roadmap to living a more fulfilling life. When I became consumed by golf, I also began to enjoy an improved existence. It may sound audacious, but I know golf can have this effect on others, too.

Anyone who is willing to give their time and concentration to golf will undoubtedly find some answers to many challenging questions. The game may not have everything you need to make positive changes, but it's one hell of a good foundation from which to build.

Golf gives me time to tinker with my personality and room to grow my good habits. When playing, I always know which direction I need to go. Sometimes that's all we need to get started on our journey toward our better selves, and who we can become.

"Sometimes that's all we need to get started on our journey toward our better selves"

A CHALLENGING PUZZLE

Right about the time you think you have golf figured out; the game will throw you a curveball. Because of its difficult nature, golf keeps us guessing. What works during one wonderful round may send you searching for balls the next time you play. It's a fickle game.

Since golf can't be mastered, it requires a lifetime of study in order to find just enough success to avoid madness. Does that sound fun? It's not a game for the easily deterred soul. Instead, it's a grand one worthy of our pursuit.

The real joy of golf comes from the journey it takes us on. Each time we walk back on to the course to find our game presents another chance that we might create a special memory. If you don't play, it won't happen.

On some level, humans crave difficulty. If golf went just right every time, we would quickly become bored with it. After all, what would be the point in trying to solve an easy puzzle?

GOLF CULTURE

The best way to improve the bottom line for a golf course is to invest in culture. The places that show a reverence for the game tend to attract golfers that do the same. The course that finds this sort of player will surely discover success.

In this scenario, it's the little things that make the biggest difference. Whether it's fun competitions, clearly communicated expectations, or even just regularly scheduled outings, it takes effort to create a compelling experience. Unfortunately, this is where most places fall short. Building culture might sound expensive, but lacking one is much more costly in the end. It doesn't take any more money to make strong impressions through service and professional pride.

Golf culture comes in many different models, but you always know it when you see it. Of course, culture is not exclusive to private clubs: some public links and municipal facilities have the best examples of culture around. It comes down to the folks that set the tone. The staff, the board, the regulars, and guests. Each personal interaction is a chance to share what a place stands for.

Anyone who comes to a golf course should be able to easily understand what matters most there and why. Some places fake it, but the true colors always shine through. Meanwhile, the best hangs are the ones where people have a high golf IQ and deep appreciation for what matters most in the game.

Show me a struggling golf course or club, and I'll show you a culture that's not what it should be. No two places are the same, but the courses that do best are ones where culture drives everything. After all, that's what golfers really come to buy.

A PURE SWING

Any time I'm faced with a must-make shot, I try to dig deep and find a pure golf swing: a swing that relies on the decades of golf experiences I've had. I don't believe it's possible to try and make a great swing. Instead, you just have to let it happen.

Our muscle memory can achieve incredible things, but first we have to get the brain out of the way. Too much thinking can disrupt our athletic ability. The best shots come from instinct. If we can visualize the result we want, focus on our setup, and let our body just react, then the result usually turns out pretty well. This is true for so many golfers.

We just have to let our swing do the work.

" you just have to let it happen "

A GOOD REASON FOR LIVING

There is no amount of money, fame, or privilege that I'd trade for the ability to play golf. My lifelong desire is to take walks with friends, make swings through fields, and stake my claim in the game I love. More obsession than habit—and more life choice than infatuation—my love for golf runs deep.

The game is woven into the very fabric of my being, and to separate me from it would fracture my soul. With each round of golf, I find myself pulled further into an unshakable relationship with the sport. As I learn from the game, I also hope to help keep it alive. I suppose that would be my way of returning the favor.

Golf is not my reason for living, it's just how I choose to do it.

SUCKER PINS

Every golfer wants to fire at the pin, but that's not always what's called for. Pardon the expression, but a "sucker pin" is named that way for a reason.

Some hole placements are meant to test restraint. When pins are tucked into corners and hidden behind hills, it may be best to hit to the middle and putt to the hole from afar. This isn't as much about playing safe as it is simply the proper way to score.

When the pin is in a diabolical position, the odds of making a birdie with a putter are much higher than with an approach shot. Pride can get in the way, though. That's what the designer and superintendent had in mind when they created certain pinnable areas.

Sometimes the exam is based more on strategy and restraint than ability. Just because you can occasionally hit it close doesn't mean you should always try to do so. When the margin for error is small, it's smart to make the target as large as possible. There's always more green to work with than the tricky pin would have you believe. Thanks to hubris, it can be harder to make the wise swing than the daring one, but we chase the sucker pin at our own peril. Instead of aiming for corners, it's better to work from the middle.

TOOLS NOT JEWELS

Golf clubs are tools, not jewels. They are supposed to get dirty, dinged up, and disheveled. Clubs only look new when they haven't been used.

They are meant to be swung through grass, mud, roots, and weeds. In that vein, wear and tear is a sign of success. You can't get dirt in your grooves unless you play, and that's what clubs are for.

Every nick on the club head is a mark of character. Those scars have stories, too. They tell of the good, bad, and ugly that happens in golf. Imperfections are indicative of adventure.

The golfer goes out into the vast expanses of the game with a goal of combatting each course: their clubs are the tools of this battle. Show me a set that lacks the blemishes and bruises brought on by regular use, and I'll show you a golfer who hasn't earned their stripes.

Those sticks are meant for hitting. Go rough them up.

LIFE IN THE ROUGH

If you play enough golf, you're going to get highly acquainted with being in the rough. That's because most of golf is a wayward experience.

The fairway is a much-preferred place to play from, but don't set your expectations there. It's better to build a game that anticipates the constant conflicts that come from difficult lies.

Much like in life, the hard spots are the norm. You best be ready to swing from such places. If you can learn to score from the difficult positions, you'll build unflappable confidence.

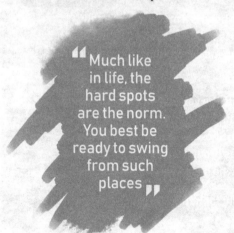

Much like in life, the hard spots are the norm. You best be ready to swing from such places

It's a lot easier to get lucky from the short grass, but the rough will make you gritty. If you can play well from there, you can succeed anywhere on the course. That's a good lesson for living, too.

A GOOD GOLF LESSON

A good golf lesson can make a mid-handicap player feel like a tour pro. With some focus on fundamentals and a pep talk on creating power, a decent player can see dramatic gains in their performance.

Those who possess a solid skill set but lack consistency are always the quickest turnaround. With a little hard work, a sensible teacher can get a higher, straighter, and more reliable shot shape from their pupil in only a few range sessions. It doesn't take long before a newfound sense of confidence kicks in.

So much of scoring comes from believing in your ability. If there's anything that makes a golf professional worth their fee, it's finding a repeatable swing that creates a confident player. Once you feel like you can take dead aim, there isn't much to stop you from shooting good scores.

CONVERSATION
BETWEEN SWINGS

Eighteen holes leaves a lot of time to talk. Especially when on foot.

When I play with my most dear companions, the conversations tend to delve into all aspects of life. We talk about family, frustrations, and even other friends. We chat about our children, current events, and career trajectory. Some people discuss their love life while others prefer the bands or shows or stocks they like. Golf trips and community gossip are always popular topics, too. There really isn't much off the table.

When I play with my pals, it's a chance to both celebrate our joys and unload some baggage. I tell my golf friends all sorts of things because through sharing, we discover we aren't alone in our successes and challenges. It's good to know others are battling similar challenges as me.

Step by step and word by word, we untangle the thoughts we tend to otherwise keep to ourselves. Perhaps it's the open space that inspires such sharing. Mostly, it's comforting just knowing that the people I walk with care enough to listen. Having someone hear me out helps more than I'd sometimes like to admit.

A tee time is a mutual agreement, in that sense. When I play golf with others, I drop my guard. The game makes everyone vulnerable, and it's that common footing that allows these discussions to happen with ease. The shots we make matter, but the talks we have along the way sometimes mean much more.

Golf is a good way to sort out where we stand with each other. There's a lot of time for conversation between swings.

A TIGHT MATCH

A tight golf match can feel like a game of chess.

When going head-to-head, it helps to watch your opponent's every move. There are signals being sent in the actions a golfer takes during competition. Some moves show confidence, while others indicate restraint. It's smart to keep a keen eye on how your opponent manages themselves during the battle.

A golf match is a contest not only of skills but also decision making. The result comes down to who can execute the best strategy. Understanding when to move your pieces—and why—makes all the difference.

SUNRISE SWINGS

Golf at sunrise is good for the soul. Taking a long walk through the morning dew helps to set a positive tone for the day. With crisp reminders of the night still lingering, the golf course wakes up to welcome golfers once again. It's a splendid time to be enjoying the gifts of this game.

There is a vibrancy to nature in those early hours. Birds, bugs, and other critters compose a symphony of stirring sounds to signal the start of something new. While the day is young, the golf is pure and unbothered. Beginning the day with such a beloved activity makes even the steepest challenges of life feel benign. For those who find their peace through golf, the dawn yields a particularly pleasing variety of the game.

Every day brings new possibilities, and playing golf is a great way to explore them. There's much to love about our world, and the course we find at daybreak is littered with those reminders. No matter the tasks that lay ahead, some sunrise swings will help keep them in perspective. It's awfully hard to have a bad day when it begins with golf.

A LOT TO SMILE ABOUT

Golf is a great way to find happiness. Even though the game is hard, it still brings a smile to thousands of faces each day. Those wide grins are caused by good shots, great friends, and grand memories. The more you play, the more you'll find of each.

Golf's popularity is derived from the game's ability to lend joy to anyone who plays it. Players of every skill level can discover rich and rewarding moments through the sport. The game is tailored to optimists, and by attracting such personalities, golf helps make the world a more delightful place.

Golf is a celebration of the small things that are worth appreciating. Every round is an opportunity to enjoy the blessings we are given. There's a lot to smile about in life, and golf is a fabulous reminder of that. To play the game is to choose to be happy.

To play the game is to choose to be happy

THE SHORT GAME

The most important part of golf to practice is the short game. It's the only element of the sport that can truly save you, no matter the situation. Well-struck wedges, bunker blasts, and consistently holed putts are the best recipe for lowering scores.

It takes time to hone those skills, though. You have to invest many hours into developing the instincts of a short-game wizard. There's no substitute for feel, and only one way to find it.

Through countless repetition, you can discover the different ways to make a ball dance. By developing a repertoire of pitch shots, you can save strokes in a wide variety of ways. The same holds true for creating a confident posture with the putter.

Short-game gains come incrementally, and then the most impressive results come all at once. After many attempts on the practice green and in play, the value of those reps starts to compound. Before you know it, the short game becomes a noticeable weapon in the war against bogey. The better it gets, the more you'll seek to practice.

SMALL MISSES

In putting, it's the small misses that sting the most. With so many factors in play on every stroke, it's hard to accept the result that comes painfully close to success. The most frustrating part is that 99 out of 100 details can be right, but it only takes one small element to keep the ball out of the hole. The ones that don't drop are tough pills to swallow.

Despite the anguish of coming so close, the near miss is a sign of many good things. The best putters have far more close calls than makes, and that constant proximity pays off over time. Putts that hang around the hole can some days fall in droves.

" the near miss is a sign of many good things "

GOLF DAYDREAMS

Do you ever find yourself daydreaming about your best days in golf? I certainly do.

Golf makes for strong and vivid memories and I often enjoy revisiting them. In my mind there exist perfect pictures of the happy days spent playing golf with family and friends on fairways near and far. Even though the rounds of my past are many years and miles behind me, I can still recall them if I close my eyes.

I can remember the details: the light, temperature, colors, firmness, foliage, and wind. In my memory I can enjoy those spectacular days again whenever I please.

With a few quiet moments and a little concentration, I can be transported to the course and with those people I love once more. I can retrace my steps and relive my swings. These recollections make me smile, but they also create a longing to plan new days for golf and record fresh memories worthy of future daydreams.

Golf is a game made for making memories and I'm someone who likes to revel in them. Every round lives on, replayed often in my heart.

THE BREAKFAST BALL

Everyone needs a breakfast ball from time to time. That first swing of the day isn't always kind. It's good to have a second ball in your pocket when you go straight to the tee box from the car.

Despite consuming copious amounts of coffee and going through a quick stretch routine, the results on the first hole some mornings can be particularly shaky. As much as I respect the rules, we need a little flexibility in certain circumstances.

Perhaps the night before is having a lingering effect on you, or it could be that you're just running terribly late: whatever the reason for your opening mulligan, don't feel so guilty. Golf is about having fun, and it's no fun to start with a failed attempt.

This won't work for tournaments and such, but for the casual round with friends and other related outings, go ahead and take a little liberty. If the first swing is good then start walking, but nobody's going to bust your chops for taking a second hack. The breakfast ball is just fine.

THE ESCAPE ARTIST

The golfer who can always find a way out is a special breed. More instinctual than well-trained, this sort of player lives on a strange see-saw.

Wayward swings bring many frowns, but the chance to wow both friends and opponents never fails to yield a smile. Whether giving it a whack from the bushes or pitching out of a ditch, the player that thinks like a magician always has a chance. Just when you think they've played their way out of a hole, they somehow find a way back in.

" the player that thinks like a magician always has a chance "

For some golfers, it's the only way they've ever known. Developing the skill needed to get out of jail is a difficult talent to acquire. Watch out for the player who grins when they hit it in the junk. Be careful not to count them out.

THE YIPS

For some reason we aren't supposed to talk about the yips. We act like it's a contagious condition, but in reality it's a problem that lives in our heads.

That's not to say the yips aren't real, because there are many examples of just how bad it can get. In the worst cases, people who have loved the game for decades choose to quit playing rather than continue through the nightmare of missing every short putt.

It may sound like just another scary story, but those who suffer through the yips can attest to the terror. Even those of us who have overcome the disorder are still affected by its lingering ghost. Such specters are hard to shake. They take hold of your thoughts and divert the club from its proper path.

It's not that the hole seems to shrink: instead, what drives people nuts is the cup is right there and they just can't hit it. For the golfer who can't afford a therapist, the only way to conquer these mental intrusions is to start over and rebuild confidence from scratch.

Often this means a new grip, putter, or perhaps an entirely different stroke. There is no one-size-fits-all solution, but there is evidence to support that this infliction can be conquered. Even still, once you have the yips, your game is forever changed.

Like anything else in golf, the yips take work to get through. They may only last a week or stay for a lifetime, but either way there will most certainly be scar tissue. It's up to the player to find a proper rehabilitation plan.

Despite the dark feelings that come with the yips, they can be overcome. Should you ever catch a bad case, don't lose hope. It's only in your head, and with some practice it'll pass.

BEING BLOWN ABOUT

When the wind picks up, those with a talent for getting the ball in the hole really shine. The short game matters greatly in any round, but especially when everyone is missing greens because of a howling wind.

Some players panic when the wind starts to blow, while others see opportunities. There is no better equalizer than the wind, and the player who can scramble tends to rise to the top.

You need imagination and concentration to be successful with the scoring clubs: a truth most evident in a gale. The player with great touch and feel is at a tremendous advantage here. When we become frustrated with the wind, those of us with a proper short game start seeing a path to victory. The person who gets up and down conquers all.

DOWN THE STRETCH

Late fall marks the final few holes of the year. It's the point in the round when I start to think about the score. Even though it's best to concentrate on the shot at hand, it's hard not to assess how things stand.

Late fall is the last chance to make a run at a good number. It's a final opportunity to turn things around. If I can finish with a flurry of good swings and perhaps make a few putts, then I may just get out of the year with my head held high.

It's not a fresh start per se, but it's a reminder that my chances to make the year special are running out. If you think about a trip around the sun like a round of golf, then you know how good it feels to make some birdies coming home. We all like to close well.

Late fall is when the final grind kicks in. It takes focus to finish strong, and the cool weather is a signal to get serious. By the time the leaves have dropped, there are only a handful of rounds left in the year. The squirrels are furiously collecting acorns, and I'm doing the same with good memories.

Late fall is about getting back on track. With a couple good shots and a decent break or two, something special could still occur. I remind myself that I can post a score that I'm proud of, but there aren't any swings left to waste.

GOLF IS EVERYWHERE

Golf is everywhere. Whether I'm on a course in person or only in my mind, the game is always there when I need it.

I use golf to sort through whatever challenges are present in my life. Sometimes that's on the course down the street or on fairways far away, but there are also occasions for which all I have is an old club and some shag balls. In that case I can make a course come to life just about anywhere.

With a little imagination and a few swings, I can conjure up some golf whenever I need it. I've found holes to play in forgotten fields and on sandy shores. Through the years, these routings have provided me great relief. Even if all I have is a few minutes to mind my thoughts, these invented golf holes help me find my way.

" the game is always there when I need it "

When the opportunity to wander around with a wedge presents itself, I'm quick to disappear. Golf was made for those whose thoughts tend to stray. The game provides me a way to channel them in productive ways.

If you see me somewhere walking with a club in hand, please know that I'm not lost. I'm just going through the process of finding my next move. The course—both real and imagined—is always calling. Most times, it takes me exactly where I need to go.

A DELIGHTFUL DOWNPOUR

I can't imagine how many times I've found myself huddled under a tree or beneath a shelter with friends during a rain delay. As much as I hate to come off the course, I still enjoy the chance to catch up with my friends when there's nowhere else to go.

While the water falls from the heavens, we find time for jokes and country club gossip. There's chatter about those with generous handicaps, opinions on the state of the course, and lots of talk about the shenanigans we all get into together. The rain pounds the ground around us and the runoff sheets over the fairways, but we are happy under our makeshift shelter.

Belly laughs and the sound of beers opening are a perfect accompaniment to the beats of a thunderstorm. We check the radar, but despite seeing shades of green and red on the screen all around us, there's no rush to go in. Why head for home when we can hide from the world right here a bit longer?

The golf course is a great place to be stranded in a downpour. Nobody is in a hurry to break the huddle.

TRAINING A GOLF DOG

Training a golf dog is serious business. It takes time, focus, and dedication from both owner and pet.

There are a great many rules that must be learned by the canine pupil. Where to stand, how to be still, when to relieve oneself, and what settings are appropriate for barking. All these details are essential in the tutelage of a young pup.

Patience is critically important. Good behavior should be rewarded with treats and other savory morsels. Poor form should be noted in a stern but considerate way. Golf dogs aren't entitled to roam free, but those who behave well should be allowed a long leash and room to stretch their legs.

The norms of the game must be obeyed, but those who wish to bring their dog should not be overly punished when a line is crossed. After all, golf is not a game of perfect. The only way to learn is to try.

Dogs have a place on the golf course. It's a wonderful thing to have them by our side while playing. A thoughtful orientation is needed, but the course should be a welcome place for our four-legged friends. Perhaps, with some training across the country, we can create golf course cultures that are better suited for such pursuits. Like anything in golf, playing with your dog is quite addictive. It just takes a little effort to get them ready to go.

THE ARTFUL DROPPER

It's never a good feeling when reaching in the bag for a new ball to put in play. Losing a ball to a hazard is both frustrating and bad for scoring. It may even feel worse to find it and be forced to take an unplayable. When we have to reach for our rule book, it's a sign of trouble.

Dropping sounds like a simple practice, but in reality it's something that requires a bit of skill. There is obviously an element of chance involved: balls do bounce, after all. The artful dropper can both find a good spot and land the ball there.

The rules for drops have changed quite a bit over the years, but it has always been something great golfers pay special attention to. The modern version is surely to the player's advantage. To release the ball from knee-high yields much better control over the end result. Good lies from the drop have become much more plentiful.

A bad drop is one of golf's worst possible results. The relief is costly to begin with, and when it results in a poor spot to play from, we feel shorted by the golf gods. With ball in hand, it's important that we get the drop right. Those are the little differences that add up when the round ends. Show me a player who carefully studies their drops, and I'll wager they have a low handicap.

THE CLUB LIFE

There are a lot of good reasons to join a golf club. The most important of which is the chance to be part of a community. Finding a proper fit is key. For me, I enjoy being able to compete with friends in an environment that's fueled by a love for the game. The friendly and competitive nature of a club is a wonderful thing to be a part of.

At our club, a shared passion for golf manifests in Tuesday skins, Friday four-ball matches, a standing game on weekends, and monthly tournaments: all of which offer an opportunity to find some small amount of fleeting personal glory. There are also endless evening walks with dogs, the site of children running around the practice green, and many good stories shared among friends.

I'm a member there because of the atmosphere we all create together. I get to laugh a lot at the club, and all our families at times seem to merge into one large unit.

Because of the culture, I spend a ton of time at our golf club. It's somewhere I always long to be. The club is a part of my life, and my life is part of the place. That's a feeling I hope every golfer can have. If you can find something similar, or another culture that suits your taste, I hope you'll dive in. There's a lot to love about a club that feels like home.

A GAME OF MISSES

The golf swing is a pretty complex operation. Hitting a great shot is not an easy thing to do. Most swings are a miss hit, and managing those results is key.

Ever since I was a boy, my grandfather has told me that golf is a game of misses. He taught me to think in terms of where to miss best, and he insisted I learn the art of recovery: both of which have shaped the way I play the game. Thanks to Gramps, I've developed a knack for thinking my way around a golf course and finding inventive ways to make par.

Appreciating the frequency of misses is also important for keeping a level head. A miss is nothing to be mad about ... it's just a situation to deal with.

"it's better to anticipate the misses and be prepared to overcome them"

Frustration will only compound the problem. Instead, it's better to anticipate the misses and be prepared to overcome them. It starts by playing better odds and missing in the right place as much as possible.

Par is often found through the path of least resistance. As Gramps would say, "a good miss can help you get where you want to go."

FIVE DOLLARS AT A TIME

There's always a match taking place at my golf club. Five-dollar Nassaus get traded more than bad jokes. Even though nobody gets rich, the stakes feel high. That's what pride will do to a golfer.

Everyone wants to be a winner. Most will never lift the club championship trophy, but they can earn the feeling of getting paid by their opponent on a weekday evening in the grill room. Abe Lincoln's face neatly folded in your wallet is a fine reward for sticking it to a friend.

It always stings, though, when you have to hand over the cash. That's why the matches matter. Having a little on the line will make you play harder.

We inflate the importance of a five-dollar Nassau in order to feel a fraction of the nerves that come from larger events. Those three-foot putts on a Thursday night might not mean much in the grand scheme, but they matter in the moment. The shots you pull off when playing against your pals become the basis for confident swings down the road. It's good to turn up the pressure. It's fun to play for money. We all get a little better five dollars at a time.

SURVIVE AND ADVANCE

There's pressure, and then there's everyone-you-know-watching-you-play-in-the-shootout pressure. I can't think of a greater challenge to an average golfer than attempting important shots in front of a large, home-club crowd. Typically reserved for member-guest events and other such competitions, the shootout is a real torture chamber for the nerves.

After a weekend of grinding through a flight of similarly skilled teams, the best of the bunch gets their shot at glory. Shootouts are composed of sorted personalities: teams that have been playing together for years, partners with business relationships, family-member squads, and obscure friendship duos all come for their chance at some cash and to put their name on a plaque.

With dozens of on-lookers surrounding each swing, it requires tremendous concentration to perform well. Every shot is riddled with tension. Make the swing, hole the putt, or face elimination. Although the challenge of winning the shootout seems daunting, someone will indeed raise their arms and achieve the unthinkable.

In the shootout there are betting favorites, lovable underdogs, and of course the ones nobody can stand. With drinks flowing and players forced to play through a raucous atmosphere, there's no telling what might happen. Usually, the day is defined by a surprise putt, an unfortunate mishap, or a momentous swing no one saw coming. That's the beauty of it.

A shootout is unpredictable, but there are always countless witnesses on hand to see how a new grill room legend unfolds. It's simply one of the best environments in golf.

A TWISTED GAME

Golfers understand agony well. This game dangles just enough hope to entice desperate fools and tightly grip a sucker's soul.

Golf is a tease. It convinces us that we too can achieve glorious things if we just keep coming back.

There are moments of splendor and many swings to be proud of, yet so much of golf is based in the crippling disappointment of "almost." This leaves thousands of players in a constant state of befuddlement. "I don't understand how..." and "why did I not just..." are both yelled and whispered each day across the golfing world. No other game can create such anguish in those who play it.

The near misses and close calls are enough to drive even the most level-headed player insane. We are regularly left to wonder "what if" while standing in the amazement of a bad break. The whole game is a big damn white whale. Much like Captain Ahab, we are forever tormented by the object of our desire and our drive for redemption, or even revenge.

The game we hope to play is always just out of reach. We know this, and yet we return time and time again, hoping that someday we just might catch what we are chasing. There's no way to stop this twisted pursuit.

ON THE SHORT SIDE

Hitting an approach shot to the short side of a tucked pin isn't a good feeling. It takes ample space to make a proper pitch. Having none doesn't bode well for the prospects of an up-and-down.

In such tight spots, hoping for a par save seems like wishful thinking. And yet, we have to try to escape. The only priority is to get a putter in hand as soon as possible. A bad chip can take par out of reach. It's best to sell out for the putting surface no matter what.

Getting to the green is essential to the save. While it may be tempting to try something risky, the prudent path is to play well past the hole. The flat stick is a much more likely hero than the wedge. With little room to operate, a wise golfer will insist on finding salvation through a long putt rather than risk falling short again.

❝ we have to try to escape ❞

There is no greater test of course management than being in a tight spot. Unfortunately, most players fail. The passing grade is awarded to the golfer who plays the odds correctly. A reasonable putt for par is all we should aim for.

WEEKEND VIBES

Golf is a fine way to ease into the weekend. A few holes, a few friends, and a few sips of something cold make for a fabulous Friday night.

Everyone needs a way to shake off the stress of a long week. I've yet to find a better system for doing so than golf.

Playing this silly game just makes my worries melt away. Whether I'm enjoying some swings with my family, walking the dog before dark, or just having a hit with my pals, there's no better way to kickstart some downtime.

There are 52 weeks in a year, and the best ones are those that end with golf. When someone needs to find me late on the eve of a weekend, the course is a good place to start the search. I'm there as much as possible, usually with a big smile on my face.

A FAMILIAR FEELING

As golfers, we all have places that move us. Some courses just draw you in. Simply being there inspires some sort of strong emotional response. Such familiar feelings bring us warm sentiments and long-lasting smiles. This is especially true in locations that have bred many fond memories with friends.

It's fun to inquire as to what course elicits these feelings from other golfers. I've found that for most players, there's one that quickly comes to mind. It can be a regular haunt or even an occasional visit, but either way the feelings are made obvious by the look in the person's eyes. You can see them go there, just for a few seconds. Then they say the name of their special place and grin from ear to ear. In that moment, we are all eager to return to the spots that fill us with joy.

When a vivid memory triggers that familiar feeling once again, it's impossible not to drift back to good swings once had on pleasant afternoons. It's remarkable that a game and a place to play it can make us feel so good. Love would not be too strong a word to describe the feeling.

THE NEXT TEE

Every golf hole is a chance to start anew. We come to the tee with big dreams and high hopes for good scores. It doesn't always work out like we planned, but as long as our head stays high and our smile is wide, everything will turn out just fine.

Through all the breaks—both good and bad—what matters most is that we keep showing up to take on the next obstacle. We must continue playing the game.

It's imperative that we face the challenge that lies ahead. We continue pressing on through the round no matter what. If we are bold in this approach, there's a good chance that fortune will find us.

That's why the next tee matters so much. If we walk up, assess the situation, and then make a confident go of it, then we have already won. This test is not graded by our results. Instead, our performance is judged by effort.

That means showing up again and again. Take the shot and go forward, to the fairway ahead and the holes beyond after that.

STRAPPED

Golf experiences don't have to be expensive or overdone. It's more than okay for a course to have flaws and a low greens fee. Yes, a cash-strapped course may leave you wanting in some regard, but as long as it provides a place for a pretty walk and some good banter with friends, then a low-key state facility will suffice.

It costs a lot of money to maintain a golf course, and instead of complaining about what isn't there, we would all be happier to simply appreciate what is. Learn to love the unkempt, the quirky, and the inconspicuous details of a place, and you'll find that any course can make you smile.

In this era of the game, with so much pressure on golf courses, it's important that we shelve our high expectations and replace them with gratitude for the chance to play. Big budgets and perfect playing surfaces yield an unnatural arena for a pastime like golf. The true spirit of the game is much rougher around the edges.

A bad lie or oddly placed tree, for example, is the sort of spice that keeps golf perpetually interesting. If a course ironed out those creases, it would be more expensive and less unique. It's a far better aim to be affordable and different from the rest.

❝ it's important that we shelve our high expectations and replace them with gratitude for the chance to play ❞

THE AIR WE BREATHE

Fresh air always helps to clear the mind. This is especially true in winter. A long walk on a crisp and cold day is a delightful refreshment for the soul. A golf course is a fine place to enjoy such bliss.

Escaping the indoors is a must during this season of shortened days and fleeting sunshine. It's a blessing to take some steps while so many others are snowbound or bundled. The swings that separate those paces are mostly just a bonus, an attractive activity between passing thoughts.

The holes played help to mark the distance traveled and give me an excuse to stay out in the elements longer than I should. A chilled air fills my lungs while a few additional layers keep me warm. It's a good time of year for this pastime, yet the forecast dictates availability. I've got plenty of thoughts to sift through, but it may be a while before I can take these deep breaths again. The walk and air are good while they last.

SEEING THROUGH THE FOG

How often do we find ourselves struggling to see the target? A fog can roll in—literal, or in our own mind—and suddenly we don't know where to aim.

It's not a scenario you can think through. It's an impasse: only your gut can guide you.

That internal compass knows the way more times than not. Its bearings come from a combination of experience, understanding, and skill. Having trust in these moments can be difficult, but whatever choice is made, it must be done with conviction.

An uncertain swing will yield a shaky result, and when blinded by the elements or our own misconceptions, we must avoid that pitfall. It's crucial to keep the vision of the target in mind, even when you can't see it.

Our powerful instincts, when buoyed by a confident decision, can take us to the desired destination. We must trust ourselves and our ability.

Quiet the mind and reconnect to your inner compass. That's the only way to steer when the clouds descend upon you.

"We must trust ourselves and our ability"

OLD FRIENDS

Every golfer needs a pal to take walks with: someone who speaks your same language and shares a similar wavelength. The course is a fine place to sort through life's challenges, and it helps to have a playing partner who listens well.

The best of friends can converse without words. They read your every move and match the mood accordingly. When the time for advice comes, sometimes they only need to flash a smile or offer a caring look. A quiet confirmation of their understanding will do just fine.

Along the walk, during the in-between times, it's this sort of companionship that yields a therapeutic benefit from golf. Knowing your buddy is near and available to hear you out means a lot. Find a friend who always says yes to golf, and you'll be on your way to an improved state of being. Especially if they have four legs and a coat of fur.

QUIET ON THE COURSE

My favorite kind of quiet is that which I find on a golf course just before night settles in.

I'm most at peace when the sky takes on a purplish tint, and the birds have sang their final songs for the day. By this time, the shadows have subsided, and the lines between light and dark become blurred. This is when my thoughts become the clearest.

These are the moments that I treasure most in golf. They are precious and fleeting. The minutes move slow, despite the quickly disappearing daylight. Found only by those who insist on chasing the last bit of golf from the day, these moments are the payoff for playing long past when the pro shop closes.

It takes a few "one last hole" declarations to find the calmness of this hour. Usually that means telling my wife I'm on the way at least once or twice while pressing past the last presence of the sun. Often there are consequences for coming home late—missing dinner, or even bedtime—but I can't help but insist on the occasional outing that lasts too long. We all need to find a few moments without friction from time to time. This is where I claim mine.

LONGING FOR GOLF

Near the end of the year, when the daylight shrinks and the frost comes back, golf starts to feel like it's slipping out of reach. The fairways turn fallow and the course goes quiet. It's a joyous season across the globe, yet the golfer arrives at a certain kind of sadness. The season is over, and despite the lack of playing opportunities, our golf dreams linger. The game still occupies our mind.

Whether at home by the fire with family, at a holiday gathering with friends, or shopping for presents in your favorite store, the thought of golf persists. With scarce daylight and busy schedules, it becomes difficult to find time for the game. You have hope for one more round, maybe two, before the year end, but it's hard to make happen. If only the days were long again.

Perhaps, if we are good boys and girls, a window to play will arrive wrapped up with a bow on it. One final gift from the golf gods before winter settles in to stay. Then again, maybe we just need the memory of sunny afternoons strolling the course with friends to keep us warm while the nights turn cold.

"A new season will start to bloom soon. Until then, we wait with hungry hearts"

It's nice to have something like that to hold on to. A happy vision for the renewed calendar ahead. While we long for golf's return, at least it gives us wonderful daydreams. A new season will start to bloom soon. Until then, we wait with hungry hearts.

HARD TO GET

Some golf courses play hard to get. They will flirt with you and make you fall in love, only to break your heart in a million little ways.

It's not one moment that leaves you wanting, it's an endless series of them. Each time you hang your hopes on an open window of opportunity, something goes terribly wrong.

All those daydreams fail to come true.

You rack your brain and ponder what happened, but really you just fooled yourself into thinking you had a chance. Perhaps that's what hurts the most.

Oddly enough, it's that same feeling that keeps you coming back. Despite the knowledge of looming disappointment, you just want to give it a go again. What got away from you once, in theory, could still be caught.

If you can only have another chance. Next time, it will be different.

THE TWO-WAY JOURNEY

Golf is a two-way journey. When you play this game, you must travel both outward and inward simultaneously.

Golf is an exploration of the land, and your journey through the round represents an ancient ritual: the walkabout. Humans are meant to venture by foot and golf is one of the last good ways to do that. You move outward from a point of origin and traverse diverse terrains while playing. It's the hike that makes golf's greatest benefits possible.

Along that wandering path, you must also venture inward. Each step offers you an opportunity to reflect on those you've already taken and the ones yet to come. Golf is a structured way to slip deeply into your thoughts and see where they take you. In this way, golf is a meditation. You can find peace through the repetition of this method.

Most scorecards describe the front and back nines as going out and in. It's a relic from the linksy origins of the game. However, those descriptors remain accurate for the greater journey. While you walk outward from the first tee and discover what each hole has in store, you also move inward through your thoughts and find new ways of understanding your true self.

When you play golf, you complete a circuitous path. Even though you come back home in the end, you never quite return to the same place. While you may be standing near your point of origin, the two-way journey ensures that the person standing there isn't the same as before.

❝ Golf is meditation ❞

THE BEST DAYS

Every day of my life has been a blessing, but the very best ones have all involved golf.

I'm at peace on the course. It's where my soul longs to be, and life just seems to make sense there. The swings and steps help me find my center.

When I play golf, my mind is engaged and my heart is full. Hope lifts my spirit, and I can see the beauty in the world more clearly. My thoughts slow down and my perspective changes for the better. I'm made happier by the game.

What's not to love about that.

END OF THE SEARCH

If you are searching for something, go play golf. I bet you'll find it.

ABOUT THE AUTHOR

Jay Revell is a golf writer for the everyman. His stories about the simple pleasures of the game have resonated with golfers around the globe. Whether blogging or writing for magazines like *The Golfer's Journal*, *McKellar*, and Golf.com, Jay has found a way to express what makes golf such a meaningful game to so many. His debut book, *The Nine Virtues of Golf*, has become a cult favorite among those who turn to golf for its meditative and therapeutic qualities. When not writing about golf, Jay loves working with clients at his marketing firm, Revell Media. He lives in Tallahassee, Florida with his wife Sarah, their daughter Winnie, son John David, and dog Leon.

Twitter: @JayRevell
Instagram: @JayRevellWrites
Website: www.jayrevell.com